BRAD BRIGHT

GOD
is the issue

Recapturing the Cultural Initiative

HATE CRIMES

TERROR

HYPOCRISY

WAR

ABORTION

AIDS

CORPORATE FRAUD

DRUGS

INJUSTICE

NewLife
PUBLICATIONS

God Is the Issue: Recapturing the Cultural Initiative

Published by
New*Life* Publications
A ministry of Campus Crusade for Christ
375 Highway 74 South, Suite A
Peachtree City, GA 30269

Design and production by Genesis Group

Cover by Larry Smith & Associates

Printed in the United States of America

ISBN 1-56399-243-4

Unless otherwise indicated, Scripture quotations are from the *New International Version*, © 1973, 1978, 1984 by the International Bible Society. Published by Zondervan Bible Publishers, Grand Rapids, Michigan.

Scripture quotations designated TLB are from *The Living Bible*, © 1971 by Tyndale House Publishers, Wheaton, Illinois.

*This book is dedicated to the man who has made the God of the Bible the issue wherever he has gone for more than fifty years. From him I learned that one's perspective on all of life's issues, big and small, is colored by one's view of God. And today, I too believe with everything inside me that God is the single issue upon which all of life hinges. I dedicate this book to the greatest man I have ever known, or ever expect to know—
my father.*

Contents

    *In focusing on effects (immoral behavior), we allow
    the true Cause of moral behavior (God Himself) to
    be sidelined in the debate, and thereby end up
    arguing over symptoms. In a relativistic "Just do
    it!" culture, "Thou shalt not . . ." cannot compete.*

    *Three reasons are given for why the church is losing
    the battle for the heart, soul, and mind of the culture:
    we lack compassion, boldness, and training. The
    church is challenged to exchange its "sword for a
    fishing pole."*

    *Practical and biblical examples are used to illustrate
    how to make God the issue. Examples are given of
    how Jesus aggressively co-opted the rhetoric of His
    opponents.*

Acknowledgments

I want to thank Michael Richardson for his help with research and his creative, fertile mind that could not think inside the box even if he so desired. I am grateful to Jim Bramlett for his research. My thanks to William Kruidenier for helping me shape my words. I owe a great debt of gratitude to Alan Sears and Richard Jefferson at the Alliance Defense Fund for keeping me out of trouble. I am very appreciative to Lynn Copeland of the Genesis Group for her advice and final edits. And a world of thanks to my friend and associate John Nill who has graciously coached me through this process.

But there are two people to whom I owe my greatest thanks. The first is my late father, Bill Bright, who over a period of months convinced me that I needed to write this book. Without his encouragement I would have never begun the process. The second is my beloved bride, Kathy, whose tremendous patience, understanding, listening skills, and encouragement gave me the time, space, and daily feedback I needed to effectively formulate my thoughts on paper. She deserves as much credit as I for this book.

Foreword

One afternoon just prior to 9/11, my younger son, Brad, dropped by the house. Sitting at the kitchen table we began chatting as we often do. And as is pretty typical in our family, the conversation soon moved to a discussion of the current state of our American culture. Our two sons, Zac and Brad, spent their growing up years exposed to a constant stream of national and world visitors through our home, listening to and participating in dialogue about God and the needs of the world around us. Now that the boys are grown and have their own families and ministries for our Lord, little has changed when we sit down together. Zac brings the thoughtfulness of a pastor/philosopher, while Brad injects the viewpoint of a former political activist now ministering with Campus Crusade for Christ.

This particular day I was exercised afresh about the terrible tragedy of the 1973 *Roe v. Wade* Supreme Court decision, which has resulted in the murder of approximately 40 million innocent unborn babies. I have several times proposed to have myself lashed to the pillars of the Supreme Court building until that horrendous ruling is rescinded. (I have never followed through with that action largely due to my beloved wife, Vonette, who shares my views concerning the evil of abortion but prayed with me for a better solution.)

"But Dad, abortion is not the real issue," Brad said.

The puzzled look on my face was an invitation for him to continue: "Abortion is just a symptom. God is the issue! Abortion, homosexuality, active euthanasia, and pornography are all just symptoms. We have let others set the agenda for us. They have framed the debate and we have been foolish enough to accept their terms of engagement. We must reframe the entire rhetorical playing field in order to make God the issue within the culture."

As Brad continued to flesh out his thoughts, the light went on! Why had I not thought of this before? As a nation, our spiritual blood has been poisoned, yet we are merely treating the boils that have resulted. In order to cure a sick culture, we must attack the root cause: the exclusion of God from American culture. "You must write your ideas down," I said to Brad.

In the months following that initial conversation, I continued to urge him to commit his ideas to writing and refine them into book form. I consider them important enough for every leader in America who follows Jesus Christ to consider. Much of what our Founding Fathers put in place still stands—a free press, individual liberty, a market economy, and so on. But without question, the greatest difference between the America of 1776 and the America of 2003 is the banishment of the God of the Bible—the God of Abraham, Isaac, and Jacob; the God and Father of our Lord Jesus Christ —from the public square. *To that fundamental flaw in the fabric of our modern culture can be traced the weakening of every moral seam since.* Only by restoring God to His rightful place as the central issue in all of human life—political, spiritual, moral, economic, philosophical—will there be sufficient motivation and reason to correct what ails America.

In the following pages Brad demonstrates the absolutely critical distinction between focusing on morality and focusing on the *source* of morality in the public square—the God of the Bible. Morality is only a symptom. God is the cause. The question we must ask ourselves is whether or not we are content to merely suppress cultural symptoms such as abortion, with varying degrees of success, or whether we really wish to cure the underlying disease. How we answer this question has major implications for how we expend our time, energies, and resources.

There are three reasons I am pleased to commend Brad's book to you: First, it is a message both Brad and I believe is from God Himself, nurtured in Brad's heart and confirmed in mine during years of observing godlessness from one coast to another in our country. Whether working with political leaders in Washington, D.C., or debating anti-God radicals on the university campus, Brad's conviction that *God is the issue* has grown deep roots and borne abundant fruit.

Second, the message of *God Is the Issue* is eminently biblical, and a message for our times. While wishing I had enjoyed Brad's insights fifty years ago in my own ministry, I can rest in the fact that God raises up His spokesmen (and spokeswomen, like Esther) to come to the kingdom "for just such a time as this." I believe this book is a sorely needed paradigm message for America, and that it comes providentially at this time.

Third, every Christian can and should apply this approach when tackling the tough moral, spiritual, and political issues facing our nation. Paradigm shifts do not happen overnight. Learning to attack the cause instead of the symptoms of moral and spiritual decay will require a reprogramming, of sorts, for today's Christian community. But the progress we make in thinking, and therefore acting, biblically about this subject will determine the kind of culture our children and grandchildren will inherit from us.

We need not settle for a "post-Christian America," or yield to the relentless onslaught against the God whose followers were instrumental in founding this great nation. As Ezekiel saw the dry bones of Israel come back to life before his eyes, we can see the soul of America revived by restoring God to His rightful place in our land—in our hearts, on our lips, in our homes, in the boardroom, in the classroom, in the marketplace, in the public square, and in the halls of government.

Brad and I are praying that God will place it upon the hearts of leaders to intentionally influence ten of millions of our fellow Americans to once again make the God of the Bible the watershed issue within our culture. It is our desire that America will *soon* say again with sincerity and authenticity, "In God we trust." We are counting on you to be a part of this God-ordained movement for His glory and praise as we seek to help our fellow countrymen once again discover the God of the Bible.

BILL BRIGHT
Founder, Campus Crusade for Christ, Int'l

Introduction

There are moments in life when we must face reality, ask the tough questions, and then choose a new course of action. I believe American Christians are at one of those crossroads in the history of our nation. The strategies of the past few decades to recapture the culture are not getting the job done. We are losing the battle for the hearts and minds of our fellow countrymen.

This book was conceived in the fall of 1992 as I sat in a pew at Hollywood Presbyterian Church listening to Dr. Lloyd Ogilvie (who went on to serve eight years as the Chaplain of the United States Senate before retiring in March 2003). His sermon that day was entitled "The Answer is God." For years I reflected on the meaning of what he said that day, and I too have come to the conclusion that the answer is God—both in street-level practice and in theory. He is the answer to every dysfunction I face as an individual, and He is the answer to every dysfunction we face as a society. If there is no God, then the questions of life are truly meaningless. In the words of King Solomon of ancient Israel, "Utterly meaningless! Everything is meaningless" (Ecclesiastes 1:2). God really is the only issue.

Since the nation's founding, many churches across America have preached consistently about the person of Jesus

Christ. That history has been punctuated by several periods of preaching on various and sundry social ills. During the decades since the moral upheaval of the 1960s, we have seen an increase in that kind of preaching again. And yet, despite our preaching, as we begin the new millennium we are confronted with a society that is shamelessly attempting to shake off all remaining vestiges of decency and morality. Society has removed God from His place at the center of everything and given Him a seat on the sidelines. And we as the church have acquiesced to their agenda, and have joined the debate over symptomatic issues instead of clarifying that God is the logical and necessary starting point for all cultural debates.

The church in America today generally communicates with the culture in one of two ways. Either we preach the straight gospel without regard to the cultural and personal context, or we simply react defensively to the symptomatic cultural ills—such as homosexual behavior, abortion, racism, or pornography. Unlike Jesus, we have a difficult time using the cultural context as a relevant platform for making the God of the Bible the issue. Therefore, God comes across as largely irrelevant to the everyday life of the average American. Consequently, the culture ends up regarding us (along with the God of the Bible) as out of touch or, worse, dangerous.

In light of this, if the Bible is true, and the God of the Bible really exists, we must conclude that we have failed to effectively communicate "God" to our culture.

My hope is that we can learn to use the symptomatic "felt" issues within our culture as springboards to address what underlies the cultural mindset in which we live and breathe—our God-belief (or lack of it). What we believe to be true about God will determine how we live and relate to those around us.

Let me say parenthetically, this book is not written for the person who intends to hold frank and open dialogue regarding the pros and cons of certain types of symptomatic behavior within the culture, such as homosexuality, premarital sex, abortion, racism, pornography, or euthanasia. Nor is it written for the person who needs to learn how to explain to his non-Christian neighbors the basics of how they may know God personally. It is not even written for the individual who is seeking to further develop an intimate relationship with God. Of course, we need to know how to do all of these things, but that is not the purpose of this book.

This book is written to the person who ardently desires to bring about wholesale change within the American cultural mindset. It is written to the person who wishes to help frame the message that could ultimately allow us to win the war, not just individual battles. It is written for the person who wants to put the "Cornerstone" (God Himself) back into His proper place as the foundation upon which the American social and moral experience will be erected once again.

It is not my intent to denigrate those who have opposed evil and fought valiantly for what is right. In fact, I applaud you and thank you from the depths of my heart and encourage you to persevere. However, despite winning many battles, we are still losing the war for the hearts and minds of our countrymen. The nation in which I am now raising my children bears more resemblance to the Sodom that Lot knew than to the America in which my father was reared. Stemming the tide is no longer enough. *We must either thrust back the tide or acknowledge defeat.* Such an effort demands a radical new plan whose elements are as old as history itself.

The bottom line is this: we need a game plan that distinguishes between cause and effect. In that process, we need tactics that allow us to foil and frustrate the opposition by using their own tools and words against them—much like Jesus did with the Pharisees. It is time to return to the basics, but in a more culturally relevant and understandable manner. Only then will we be able to ultimately win the culture war, by making the God of the Bible the central issue within the culture. Debating the issues apart from the larger context of God Himself is the practical equivalent of rearranging the deck chairs on the Titanic while it sinks beneath the waves. There is no longer any other way to win.

My desire is that this book will help us all along that path —laypersons, pastors, visionaries, strategists, ministry leaders, businessmen, and politicians. I hope it will help us frame the "God" issue in a way that our fellow Americans can more readily understand and accept. I trust it will help us to recapture the soul of America so that we may become the "shining light on a hill" that was the dream of our forefathers. I pray that, along with the sons of Issachar in 1 Chronicles 12:32, we too may understand our times and know what to do.

CHAPTER 1

Identifying Cause and Effect

"If there is no God, then everything is permitted."
FYODOR DOSTOEVSKY

America, the noble experiment, is under siege. The nation that once aspired to being a shining light on a hill is now one of the world's leading exporters of pornography. The nation that was once a haven for religious refugees now seeks to exclude religious speech from education and the public square. The nation that once paid the blood price to free its slaves now freely spills the blood of its young on the altar of "choice." Religious belief, once revered, is now publicly reviled. The foundation of all that most of us once held dear as a nation has so eroded that it can no longer stay the culture.

Many have worked diligently for decades in order to hold back the tide of evil in America. We all owe those individuals a great debt of gratitude and our continuing support. My prayer is that God will continue to strengthen their hands for the tasks He has given them. However, every year that goes by we continue to lose more ground. For every step we take forward, we seem to take two steps back. The time has now come for a new plan.

The primary remedy is not simply to restore "traditional values." Although it is helpful, it is no longer enough. As a nation we have gone so far down the road of relativism that the foundation that once supported traditional morality is now largely eroded. Values, while very important, are merely symptoms, or effects. Therefore, we must not only attempt to restore values, but must deal with the underlying cause of their erosion, or else all is ultimately for naught.

The father of our country, George Washington, understood this very well when he stated:

> Reason and experience both forbid us to expect that national morality can prevail in exclusion of religious principle.[1]

He also said:

> It is impossible to rightly govern the world without God and the Bible.[2]

Our first president knew that the basis of morality is God—specifically, the God of the Bible. Without Him, "national morality" cannot prevail, because there will be no rational foundation for it.

The words of our second President, John Adams, are also profound:

> Our Constitution was made only for a moral and religious people. It is wholly inadequate to the government of any other.[3]

If Washington and Adams were correct in their assessment, cultural conservatives need to take the next logical step in order to effectively turn the battle. We must become skilled at distinguishing between *cause* and *effect*. We must begin focusing more of our efforts on curing the disease instead of just treating the cultural symptoms. If we fail in this regard, it will be to our own detriment both as individuals and as a nation.

Some within our ranks have already begun to understand this while many others still have not. Following the September 11th attacks on the World Trade Center and the Pentagon, some of our religious leaders laid the blame at the feet of the homosexuals, radical feminists, abortionists, pornographers, and other misguided groups of blind sheep. However, on September 13, two days after the bombings, Jane Clayson on CBS's "The Early Show" interviewed Anne Graham Lotz, the daughter of Billy Graham. Jane asked her, "If God is good, how could God let this happen?" Anne's response nailed the cause dead center:

For several years now Americans in a sense have shaken their fist at God and said, "God, we want you out of our schools, our government, our business; we want you out of our marketplace." And, God, who is a gentleman, has just quietly backed out of our national and political life, our public life, removing His hand of blessing and protection.[4]

Anne's response reflected a clear understanding of the difference between cause and effect, between disease and symptom. She understood that the core issue is our nation's rejection of the God of the Bible from the public square.

Her observation is clearly illustrated by a *Time* magazine article entitled "The Conservative Case for Gay Marriage" (June 30, 2003). The most telling statement of the article was, "As for religious objections, it's important to remember that the issue here is not religious." Translation: religious belief (and therefore, God) has no place at the table when making public policy regarding moral issues.[5]

Like Anne Graham Lotz, Margaret Sanger, the founder of Planned Parenthood, also understood this cause and effect relationship as reflected by her statement:

> Birth control appeals to the advanced radical because it is calculated to undermine the authority of the Christian churches. I look forward to seeing humanity free someday from the tyranny of Christianity.[6]

Sanger's ultimate goal was not to promote birth control. Rather, she ardently desired to "undermine" the authority of the church in a "calculated" manner. Birth control was merely the means, the vehicle, the tool. The end, or the goal, was undermining Christianity.

Aldous Huxley, author of *Brave New World*, clearly explained man's dilemma in *Ends and Means*: "The philosopher who finds no meaning in the world is not concerned exclusively with a problem in metaphysics. He is also concerned to prove that there is no valid reason why he personally should not do as he wants."[7] Aldous Huxley may have said the words, but Adolph Hitler and Joseph Stalin gave them their horrific and logical expression.

The damning and prophetic words of Aleksandr Solzhenitsyn, spoken twenty-seven years ago in an address over the BBC radio network, have come back to haunt us. Accusatorially summing up the mentality of the West during the 20th century, he stated, "Since there are no higher spiritual forces above us and since I—Man with a capital M—am the crowning glory of the universe, then if anyone must perish today, let it be someone else, anybody, but not I, not my precious self, or those who are close to me."[8] We have pushed God aside and focused on self. And as we have pragmatically focused on self, we have lost the unpragmatic ability to "love our neighbor"—a necessary element of morality. (It is no accident that Jesus said, in Matthew 22:35–40, that the two universal laws on which all others hang are, first, to love God, then to love one's neighbor. If there is no God, there is no motivation for loving one's neighbor.)

It is now time to recognize with Anne Graham Lotz, Aleksandr Solzhenitsyn, and many others that *moral collapse is not the critical issue.* It is no more than a symptom of a deeper problem. Therefore, to allow abortion, homosexual behavior, or any other moral issue to continue to dominate the debate is akin to focusing on patching the cracked walls of a building constructed on a crumbling foundation. A discerning person will quickly correct the problem with the foundation. Otherwise he will be patching the walls right up to the day that the foundation finally gives way and the entire structure collapses—patches and all.[9]

When my child comes to me with a skinned knee, a Band-Aid is a good solution. When a friend is diagnosed with heart disease, a Band-Aid is no longer adequate. America now has heart disease. Merely treating the symptoms is no longer enough.

In the Bible, Jesus told the story of two men. One man built his house on a foundation of rock, the other man built his house on sand. One house withstood the storms, the other collapsed (Matthew 7:24–27). Trying to restore "traditional values" or "biblical values" in our nation without restoring the foundation of those values is like the man who built his house on a foundation of sand.

We must begin rebuilding the foundation by making the God of the Bible *the* watershed issue of life. He must become the dividing line of the culture. Not everyone must believe in the God of the Bible. Not everyone must be a follower of Jesus or believe the Bible is true. But the God of the Bible *must* become the issue on which everyone has a strongly felt opinion. This will allow us to control the rhetorical playing field. And as any good debater understands, if you can control the rhetorical playing field, you are almost guaranteed victory in the end. Both the apostle Peter and the apostle Paul modeled this for us in the Book of Acts as they made Jesus the watershed issue wherever they went. Like them, we dare not be ignored on this one issue. To be ignored necessarily means failure. To be sidetracked ultimately means defeat. If we fail at this task, we will ultimately fail at all other related tasks.[10]

If we continue to solely debate "behavior" in the current cultural vacuum of moral relativism, we cannot win the war.

If we continue to solely debate "behavior" in the current cultural vacuum of moral relativism, we cannot win the war. We will win some battles due to the pragmatic nature of many of our arguments, but never the war. For instance, pragmatism often helps us to promote abstinence because it is clearly the most effective means of preventing unwanted pregnancies and sexually transmitted diseases. However, it hurts us in opposing stem cell research on human embryos. Pragmatism says that because they are going to be discarded anyway, we should use those embryos for research to try to help other people.[11] Although being pragmatic is often effective, we must be ever mindful that pragmatism is a fickle ally.

We must face the reality that in most cases our argument does not "feel" as good. In a relativistic culture, "Thou shall not...," cannot compete with, "Just do it!" Even the Bible is clear that sin *is* pleasurable for a time (Hebrews 11:25). Why would people deny themselves a single pleasure if, from their perspective, the God of the Bible really does not exist or is irrelevant to everyday life?

However, switch the starting point of the cultural debate from *behavior* to *God* and victory becomes a real possibility. This is because it is rationally impossible to begin with the premise "God" (as defined by the Bible) and end with the conclusion that any immoral behavior is acceptable. Why else has the other side worked so hard to remove "God" from the public square, beginning with public education?

Let me illustrate. While ministering with Campus Crusade for Christ at the University of Washington, our student leaders decided to hold a debate on moral relativism. I went to one of the professors in the Philosophy Department who was known to be an atheist to ask if he would debate the position that moral absolutes do not exist. After he finished laughing at me, he said that even though relativism is the philosophy of the masses, no philosophy professor who had any brains would debate in support of it because it was an intellectually bankrupt theory. I was shocked to hear this statement from a secular philosophy professor who was a known atheist! He advised me to go to the Literature Department where I should have no problem finding a "wacko" who would gladly take up the cause.

But the most profound statement he made is that "absolutes are self-evident." By this he clearly meant that moral absolutes must exist in the universe. However, his problem was that he had been unable to develop a rational argument justifying the existence of absolutes apart from God's existence. Of course, this is always the insurmountable problem for those who have an inadequate or nonexistent God-concept. "God" really is our trump card.

However, I do not believe that we can approach the process of talking about the God of the Bible in the traditional manner and expect to succeed. God-fearing people have worked hard to stem the tide of evil and yet abortion is firmly entrenched. Racism still pervades society, including the church. Tolerance reigns supreme in the university. The active euthanasia movement advances, under the mantra of "death with dignity," and pornography continues to tighten its death grip on us (according to James Dobson, about 40 percent of all U.S. pastors are addicted to pornography).[12] Biblical Christians have become increasingly marginalized and irrelevant to the culture. Some leading pro-morality activists have in effect said that we have lost, so we should just take our toys, go home, and ride out the storm. Even Aleksandr Solzhenitsyn withdrew from the public arena in order to write for future generations since in his opinion we had already lost the culture war with no hope of regaining the advantage in our lifetimes.

The ultimate debate is not about changing societal behavior. Rather, it is about the person of God Himself.

The situation is bleak and the current strategy is not getting the job done. *We need to develop a new game plan. We need a new set of blueprints. We need a different map.*

Two final points of clarification are needed here. First, we must keep in mind that the ultimate debate is not about changing societal behavior. Rather, it is about the person of God Himself. As a culture, our behavior will necessarily be determined by our underlying God-belief.

Second, many would contend that the church in America *is* faithfully proclaiming the Word of God, thereby making God the issue. But if that is true, why do only 9 percent of all "born again" teens believe in absolute moral truth?[13]

(That means 91 percent of "born-again" teens do not believe in absolute moral truth.) Why do 40 percent believe that Jesus sinned?[14] Why do 68 percent not believe that the Holy Spirit is real?[15] Why do 53 percent believe that all faiths teach equally valid truths?[16] Why do 78 percent of all students in private religious schools consider it acceptable to cheat on exams?[17] Why do 95 percent think it is okay to lie to their parents?[18] If American teens who have grown up in the church had a proper view of God, we would not see such statistical symptoms. Based on this and much more data, we can reasonably conclude that the church today has failed to effectively communicate biblical truth about God —at least to young people (and the research on adults is not much more encouraging). This is true for a number of interrelated reasons, which we will explore in the next chapter.

In this regard, Oswald Chambers writes in *My Utmost for His Highest*, "Conscience is that faculty in me which attaches itself to the highest that I know, and tells me what the highest I know demands that I do. It is the eye of the soul which looks out either towards God or towards what it regards as the highest, and therefore conscience records differently in different people."[19]

Our view of God will determine our belief system as individuals and as a society. It will determine whether we believe in sexual preference or the sanctity of God-ordained marriage. Will I demand "my rights," or do I fulfill my God-given responsibilities toward others? Do I talk about "death with dignity" or life with transcendent meaning? Is it merely a fetus, or is it a person created by God in His image? Will we, in the sarcastic words of philosopher Friedrich Nietzsche, "cry at the grave of God," or will we with the shepherds and the wise men bow at the manger?

God is the watershed. If we fail to make God the issue, we shall most certainly and inevitably fail on every other cultural front. Time is not on our side and neither is the culture. If we fail to make God the issue now, even greater personal sacrifice will be required in the future.

Review Questions

1. George Washington said, "It is impossible to rightly govern the world without God and the Bible." What results do you see in our culture of attempting to govern America without the influence of God and the Bible?

2. Apply Washington's statement to your personal life. What differences do you see when you allow God and the Bible to "govern" your life? Why does national moral health begin at the personal, individual level?

3. In your own words, describe the difference between focusing on symptoms and focusing on causes. Why are discussions about symptoms irrelevant if there is no discussion about cause?

4. List five problems America faces which are symptomatic of a failure to acknowledge God. For each problem, identify the aspect of God's character or a corresponding biblical principle which could have kept that problem from arising had it been acknowledged or obeyed.

5. What have you done in the past, or what can you do in the future, to make God the main issue in your life? In your community? In your state? In our nation?

CHAPTER 2

Communicating God's Heart

"For God so loved the world that he gave…"
JESUS (JOHN 3:16)

Today, although the doors of the churches in this nation are still wide open, we are losing the battle for the hearts and minds of our fellow Americans. I believe this is true for a number of reasons, but I will address only three in this chapter.

Lack of Compassion

First, our hearts often do not truly reflect God's heart. We focus on symptoms, but God focuses on the cause. We tend to judge others based on their outward appearance. God always judges based on the heart.

A few years ago, a friend of mine, John (not his real name), was having problems in his marriage. One day his pastor stopped by unannounced and in no uncertain terms made it clear that John needed marriage counseling. After hearing what his pastor had to say, John explained the true problem: he was not following God closely and no amount of marriage counseling would do any good until he decided to put God first in his life. He rebuked the pastor for not having even asked about his spiritual condition. John instinctively understood that a person cannot follow Jesus Christ and be consistently self-centered—the primary cause of his marital troubles. I suspect the pastor was reminded that day of the importance of looking beyond the symptoms.

I did not have God's heart. I did not even begin to grasp God's overwhelming compassion for all of humanity.

I have to keep this in mind myself. When I was younger, I was extremely judgmental of people who engaged in certain types of immoral behavior. In fact, I was clear that I wished those people would just go away forever. I now cringe inside as I recall this because my words certainly did not come from the God of the Bible who said, "Love your neighbor." Nor did they reflect the words of Jesus in the story of the Good Samaritan. Fortunately, a number of years ago, a long-time family friend gently pulled me aside and gave me wise counsel. He graciously complemented me on having a clear understanding of "right and wrong." Then he said, "But, Brad, you do not have the gift of compassion. Whatever you do in life, surround yourself with people who have the gift of compassion and ask for their counsel." In retrospect, I understand that what he was saying with great diplomacy was that I did not have God's heart. I did not even begin to grasp God's overwhelming compassion for all of humanity. Jesus Christ died for everyone. Who did I think I was to wish that anyone would die in his sins—and spend eternity in hell separated from his Creator?

My former lack of compassion for the lost is unfortunately not an anomaly in the church today. I wish I could say that among those who claim to follow Jesus such thinking is rare. But sadly, I cannot. I wish I could say that my fellow Christians really embraced in their heart of hearts the sentiment, "Hate the sin, but love the sinner." But sadly, I cannot. I wish I could say that we live out the command, "Love your enemies. Do good to those who hate you." But sadly, I cannot.

A number of years ago, after my wife and I moved to a new city, we began looking for a church home. One Sunday we visited one of the more prominent churches in the area. That particular morning the pastor related how he had been out sailing the previous week with friends. Upon returning to the dock at the end of the day, he observed a rather weather-beaten character sitting on the dock reading his Bible. However, on closer inspection he saw a cigarette dangling from the man's mouth. And then, when a boat being removed from the water slid off its trailer and scraped on the concrete ramp, the man spewed forth a string of expletives.

At this point my mind raced to the story in the Book of Acts where Philip was sent by the Spirit of God out into the desert; there he crossed paths with an Ethiopian royal official who was reading the Scriptures without understanding, as the man on the dock appeared to be. Recognizing this, Philip explained the Scriptures to him, and after the man embraced Jesus as God's son, Philip baptized him.

However, to my absolute shock, the pastor told his people that he walked away from the profane man burning with anger as he went. He looked down at the congregation, full of "righteous indignation," giving vent to his outrage, berating any in the sanctuary who might exhibit similar behavior. I was stunned. Not only had this pastor missed a tremendous opportunity to encourage a person in his search for God, but he had taught his congregation, in so many words, to do the same.

The next week we returned to the same church, only to hear the pastor tell another story about a drunk driver who had killed a mother and her child that past week. His words were scathing as he heatedly condemned the man. Once again, I felt as though someone had sucker-punched me. Yes, the drunk driver had done a horrible thing for which he should be punished by the state. However, a person who had just inadvertently killed a mother and her child would probably be in the midst of intense emotional distress and therefore incredibly open to receiving God's forgiveness—if he only understood how.

I can only wish that the pastor had asked for volunteers from the congregation to go with him to minister to the man "with a cup of water" in the name of Jesus during his time of self-inflicted anguish. It would have been a natural moment to communicate God's incredible love and mercy. Another opportunity missed.

I am sure this pastor meant well, but like we are all prone to do, he focused on condemning the symptom rather than confronting the underlying cause. All of us, Christians and non-Christians alike, need to experience God's unconditional love and forgiveness because of our sins. That is what gives us hope. Through this forgiveness we receive the life of Christ —the foundation for real change, both individually and corporately.

Is it any wonder that the world hates Christians? We often speak of God's condemnation, while neglecting to extend His love and forgiveness. We reject people because they are sinners. Yet that is exactly why they need God's forgiveness—because they are sinners. After all, we may be saved by grace, but let us never forget that we too have sinned. Even the apostle Paul claimed to have been the "worst of sinners" (1 Timothy 1:15,16). Jesus came to heal the sick, not the healthy. He came to seek and to save the lost. Jesus also told us to take the log out of our own eye first before we try to take the speck out of someone else's (Matthew 7:3–5). It would be one thing if the world hated us because they saw Jesus in us. However, I fear we are often hated because they do not see Jesus in us at all—rather they see only self-righteous "Pharisees" all too eager to cast the first stone.

We should heed the words of Jesus when He accused the religious leaders of His day of being "hypocrites" and "whitewashed tombs, which look beautiful on the outside but on the inside are full of dead men's bones" (Matthew 23:27).

In Revelation chapter 2, Jesus commends the church in Ephesus because their deeds were great, they worked hard, and they did not tolerate wickedness in their midst; yet He had a complaint against them: they had left their "first love" for Him. Jesus said that the entire Law and the Prophets hang on the two commands to love God and love others (Matthew 22:37–40). The apostle Paul is very clear that if we do not have love, our deeds amount to nothing at all from God's perspective:

> If I speak in the tongues of men and of angels, but have not love, I am only a resounding gong or a clanging cymbal. If I have the gift of prophecy and can fathom all mysteries and all knowledge, and if I have a faith that can move mountains, but have not love, I am nothing. If I give all I possess to the poor and surrender my body to the flames, but have not love, I gain nothing (1 Corinthians 13:1–3).

Whenever God gives me the privilege of mentoring believers, I make it very clear that they will hear very little about behavior, but a lot about having a heart for God. Is this because behavior is unimportant? No! In fact, behavior is extremely important because it is an effective indicator of where the heart is. I watch behavior carefully (including my own), because behavior always follows belief. If behavior does not begin to change over time, there is usually still a heart problem that needs to be addressed. Simply put, I prefer to focus on treating the cause rather than the symptoms.

Joel Hunter is the pastor of the church we now attend in Orlando. Like Philip in the Book of Acts, Joel is a man who has God's heart, and distinguishes between cause and effect. One Easter Sunday a couple of years ago, as the crowds were waiting to enter the church, Joel observed a number of people cursing and smoking. Instead of taking offense, he got excited because he knew such behavior was an indicator that there would be many in the audience that day who needed to hear that God loves them and offers forgiveness, and he would have the privilege of telling them how they could receive it.

If behavior does not begin to change over time, there is usually still a heart problem that needs to be addressed.

What a contrast! On the one hand is the pastor I mentioned earlier who focuses on outward behavior and condemns not only the sin but also the sinner. On the other hand is a pastor who understands what the outward behavior really means—it is merely a symptom. Although God's condemnation is very real, His love is absolutely overpowering. God's heart's desire is for reconciliation, not condemnation. That must be our heart's desire also.

41

Lack of Boldness

This leads to the second reason why we are losing the battle for the souls of our fellow citizens. In the church today, we spend the majority of our time sitting around the campfire, holding hands, and singing "Kum Ba Yah." We often forget that we are also to stand up and march out singing "Onward Christian Soldiers." (I mean this metaphorically, of course.) Most of us do not even attempt to communicate with the culture. We mistakenly (or conveniently) think it is the job of preachers and "full-time" Christian workers to evangelize.

While at the University of Washington, one of my fellow team members went to the student body president and asked him if anyone had ever taken a few minutes to explain to him how he could know God personally. The president responded by saying, "No, a number of my friends have had the opportunity but no one has ever taken it." (In other words, he knew that a number of his friends were Christians, but none of them had ever bothered to tell him how to begin a relationship with God.) His response reflects one of the primary problems we face in the church today: More often than not, we fail to even attempt to engage the culture in dialogue about who God is.

Once a young Christian I was mentoring told me that evangelism was just a "Campus Crusade for Christ thing." He said that it certainly was not a directive for all believers. After I picked my jaw up off the floor, I suggested that we do a study of the Book of Acts. A few weeks later the young man sheepishly acknowledged that he had been wrong. It was a joy to see him begin to blossom as he followed the example of Peter, Paul, and even Jesus Himself as he took advantage of opportunities to tell his peers about God's love and forgiveness.

Over the years I have had many people say to me, "Your father must have the gift of evangelism." Frankly, I am not convinced that he does. But I am convinced that he has God's heart of compassion for those who do not know the Creator God. When he receives a telephone call that is a "wrong number," he tells the caller about Jesus. He talks about Jesus to taxi cab drivers, CEOs, bag boys, flight attendants, hotel maids, doctors, nurses, criminals, lawyers, and politicians. Growing up, whenever we went on family vacations, we would often realize Dad was missing and turn around to see him talking with someone we had passed twenty yards earlier. It is important to understand that this is a man who is rather reserved by nature. He is not an extrovert by anyone's account. But he wants people to know the God that he knows. Even my six-year-old son knows the heart of his grandfather. Recently a salesman visited our home. My son's first words to him were, "My grandfather has told billions of people about Jesus." That may not be the literal truth, but it certainly reflects his heart.

One of the worst excuses I have heard for not even attempting to tell others the good news about God's love is the statement, "I do not have the gift of evangelism." If such an excuse is legitimate, then I should be excused from having to show compassion since I do not have that "gift" (as I mentioned earlier). I am sorry if this seems offensive, but it needs to be said. *If we are not willing to talk about the one issue that is foundational to morality itself, we have no right to complain as the moral state of the nation continues to disintegrate.*

Lack of Training

The third reason we are losing the battle for the heart of America is this: Even when we do step outside of our comfort zone and tell others about God's love and forgiveness, most of us do not know how to effectively communicate with our non-Christian peers. We often use words like "grace," "salvation," "born again," "sinner," or even "Christian." These are all good words if properly understood, but in many cases we might as well be speaking ancient Hebrew to our fellow citizens. When we move out of the church into the culture and we continue to speak our "in-house" language, it is not only unintelligible to the unchurched, but it can make them feel like outsiders. They cannot understand us, and therefore we are ineffective messengers.

While in politics in Washington, D.C., I remember asking an associate if he was a "Christian." Because of his Southern Bible-belt background he responded, "Of course, I am! What do you think I am, a Communist?!" With my West Coast upbringing, it had never occurred to me that someone would think in those terms. I have since learned that

"Christian" can have a number of *perceived* meanings in our culture, a few of which are not even remotely positive—or accurate. And if the word "Christian" is misunderstood, do we really think words like "sin" or "salvation" are going to be properly understood?

If I want to communicate with Brazilians, I learn to speak Portuguese. If I want to address a businessman on Wall Street, I use illustrations from the world of finance and wear a conservative suit. If I want to communicate with young children, I keep my vocabulary and choice of topics simple. When we do not understand our audience, we will at best fail to communicate. At worst, we can even come across as stupid, unloving, mean-spirited, intolerant, or hateful— despite our good intentions. Part of being a good messenger is learning how to shape our message so our audience can understand us. (I will deal with this more extensively in the following chapters.)

A few years ago, my wife and I lived next door to two homosexual men, Bill and Rob. They were nice guys and we would chat with them as occasion permitted. One evening as I was working in our garage, Bill stopped by after work to talk. Knowing I was a Christian, he began making statements clearly trying to provoke a negative reaction. However, I simply turned to him and graciously asked, "Bill, are you a Christian?" He looked at me a bit perplexed and then emphatically responded, "No!" To which I calmly replied, "Then I won't expect you to act like one." His behavior was not the primary issue, and he needed to understand that so we could then move to the underlying causal issue—his God-belief.

While I was single, I went out of town for a few days and returned to discover I had left raw hamburger on the counter. It was full of disgusting, wriggling maggots and the stench was overwhelming. I often think of that experience as I observe the moral decay of our culture. When meat is left out on the counter, should I be surprised when it rots? If a blind person bumps into me, should I be surprised or offended? Of course not! Likewise, when a person does not believe in the God of the Bible or has a misconception about who God is, why should I be surprised when he behaves as if the God of the Bible does not exist? That person is merely behaving in a manner consistent with his very nature.

Attempting to correct wrong behavior while ignoring underlying belief is shortsighted and ultimately destined to fail.

In the church we often confuse the symptom with the disease—the effect with the cause. We condemn a pagan for behaving like a pagan. Why would we expect a pagan to act any other way? Instead, we must help effect a change in that person's God-concept. If this occurs, then his outward behavior should naturally change over time to reflect the new belief. In all of the apostle Paul's missionary trips, he never pleaded with pagans to change their outward behavior. Rather, he sought to convince them regarding the identity of Jesus Christ as God. Why? Because behavior is merely a symptomatic reflection of our God-belief. This is true for both the non-Christian *and* the Christian. If the behavior is wrong, we should take a close look at the underlying God-concept. Attempting to correct wrong behavior while ignoring the underlying belief is shortsighted and ultimately destined to fail. It is simply another form of behavior modification.

In Luke 19:10, following His encounter with a *hated* tax collector named Zacchaeus, Jesus was very clear that He came to "seek and to save what was lost." Why should our agenda be any different? Jesus said, "Follow me, and I will make you fishers of men" (Matthew 4:19). Are we fishing, or are we scaring the fish away? We are called to be messengers effectively extending God's heart of love and forgiveness to a hurting world, and not merely "Teachers of the Law." It is time for many of us to exchange our sword for a fishing pole. For others of us it is time to actually learn how to bait our own hook.

In the following chapters we will explore some ways in which our words may become more relevant to the culture surrounding us.

Review Questions

1. Cite a time in your life when you have drawn your emotional and rhetorical "sword" in an effort to judge or repudiate the behavior of some in our culture. Cite a time when you took out your "fishing pole" in an effort to reach them. How do you explain the difference in your motivation?

2. What evidence would you cite that shows your heart reflects God's heart for "sinners" in our culture?

3. What national or social issues do you pray about on a regular basis?

4. How bold are you in making God's perspective known to neighbors, coworkers, or civic leaders? What price, if any, have you had to pay for your boldness?

5. To what degree is lack of knowledge or training an issue in your willingness to take a stand for God's perspective in our culture? What kinds of training do you need in order to be more effective?

CHAPTER 3

Reframing the Issue

"Give to Caesar what is Caesar's, and to God what is God's."
JESUS (MATTHEW 22:21)

Great communicators and leaders know that, to be effective, they must first develop their message and then stay focused on their message no matter what. This was illustrated in 1994 at the University of Washington in Seattle. That fall term clearly demonstrated the importance and effectiveness of staying on message without deviation.

During the second week of school, Todd, a student, came up to an information table that Campus Crusade for Christ had set up in front of the dorms. His first question was, "Can I sign up for a Bible Study?" The college coed sitting behind the table, of course, responded affirmatively. His follow-up question came more to the point. "I'm gay. Can I still sign up?" The young woman again responded with an unequivocal, "Yes, we would love for you to join us." That was probably not the answer he expected. Finally, he asked, "Is there anything I would not be allowed to do because of being gay?" Her next response finally gave him what he had wanted all along. As graciously as she knew how, she explained that due to biblical prohibitions he could not hold any position of leadership in ministry as long as he engaged in homosexual behavior. His all too familiar parting mantra was, "I'm offended."

The next day, the front page of *The Daily* (the student newspaper) read "Christian group won't allow gay students to be leaders."[20] The following edition featured an editorial entitled "Why is CCC's discrimination condoned by UW?"[21] There was a call to revoke Campus Crusade's charter as an officially recognized student organization. It was a classic setup.

Our response was not to cower but to confront. However, we refused to do so on our opponents' terms. The following week we handed out 10,000 flyers at all the major foot traffic points leading into campus. The flyer never used the words "homosexuality" or "homosexual"; rather, it made reference to "a small, vocal minority." Most students knew who we meant, but we did not want to do anything to distract from our ability to aggressively co-opt and control the rhetorical initiative. We wanted to reframe the issue as "censorship" rather than intolerance. If we had used the word "homosexuality" it would have watered down the focus of our message. We then accused the "small, vocal minority" of being hypocritical, of undermining true diversity, of seeking to ban free speech, and of practicing censorship. The first step was to put them in a defensive posture.

We then ended the front page of the bifold flyer with the question, "What are they afraid you might hear?" This allowed us to segue into our issue: the God of the Bible and Jesus Christ. It also allowed us to wrest control of the rhetorical playing field.

For the next three months our opponents attacked, calling us homophobes and bigots, while *we strategically ignored their issue*. We countered by accusing them of *censorship*, thereby putting them right back in a defensive posture. We then continued, following up with the question, "What don't they want you to hear?" allowing us to again talk about our issue—God. We wanted to debate cause, not effect. We understood that treating symptoms while ignoring the underlying disease is shortsighted.

For the entire fall semester the militant homosexuals gave us a platform, which we gratefully accepted. However, they finally figured out two things: first, that under no circumstances were we going to be so foolish as to talk about their agenda—homosexual behavior; and second, that *every* time they attacked they were going to be accused of censorship. The strategy kept them in an untenable defensive posture, while simultaneously giving us the opportunity to talk about our issue—Jesus Christ.

Finally, in December, they went away with one final, frustrated whimper from the opinion editor of *The Daily*, a self-acknowledged homosexual. They realized they were doing themselves no favors. Not only were they expending a lot of effort and not making any headway, they were actually losing ground. We were hammering them about censorship while ignoring the homosexual issue. And by talking about Jesus Christ, we were actually undermining their position. One cannot reasonably embrace the God of the Bible while engaging in behavior that the Bible deems immoral.[22]

Allow me to parenthetically touch on a relevant issue. Some people try to argue that the God of the Bible does not condemn homosexual behavior, despite the fact that every clear biblical reference to such conduct is, *without exception*, negative. There is *not even one* clear statement regarding homosexuality in the entire Bible that is positive. Not one! (If every statement I make about spinach is negative, then an intelligent person will soon come to the conclusion that I do not like spinach.) In light of this, the burden of proof is heavy indeed upon those who say that the Bible condones homosexual behavior in any way, shape, or form.

The strategy we used at the University of Washington is not new. In Matthew 22, the Pharisees came to Jesus and asked Him if it was lawful to pay taxes to Caesar. They were trying to set Him up just as the "inquiring" university student had done to us. If Jesus said, "No," He would risk arousing the ire of the Roman ruling establishment. If He said, "Yes," the masses, which passionately hated their foreign overlords, might turn against Him. Therefore, instead of answering the question, Jesus accused His opponents of being "hypocrites," thereby attacking their credibility in an area in which they were vulnerable and putting them on the defensive. (This is the same tactic we used at the university by legitimately accusing our opposition of censorship and hypocrisy.)

Jesus then followed up by reframing the question: Since the money the Jews used bore the image of Caesar, was it not his? If so, was it right to withhold from Caesar what was rightfully his? But Jesus did not leave the discussion there—His real goal was not to settle an issue about money, but to point people to God. Therefore, immediately after telling them, "Give to Caesar what is Caesar's," He added, "and to God what is God's" (Matthew 22:21). He did not just address the issue at hand—man's obligation to the state. Rather, He used the opportunity to springboard into the greater issue of man's obligation to God. In the process He also exposed the Pharisees' hypocrisy. They weren't concerned about whether or not they should pay taxes (any more than the inquiring college student was actually interested in leading one of our Bible studies). The Pharisees' goal was to maintain their own power by discrediting someone they viewed as a threat. But when Jesus took the initiative and changed the terms of the debate, the same thing occurred as ultimately happened at the University of Washington: "they left ... and went away" (v. 22). When God becomes the central issue, debates about secondary matters often take care of themselves and even go away.

Matthew chapter 21 records how the religious leaders came to Jesus seeking to corner Him by inquiring about the source of His authority. They hoped to either trap Him into claiming equality with God so they could stone Him, or rhetorically undermine the basis of His authority. However, Jesus made it clear that if they wanted Him to answer their question, they would first have to answer a question for Him regarding the source of authority of John the Baptist: was it God or man? Whichever way they answered His question, they were going to look bad. Jesus put them in a lose/lose situation while making God the pivotal issue in the debate about the source of legitimate authority. Again, Jesus had turned the rhetorical tables, and made God the issue.

Jesus consistently and skillfully reframed the question so as to stay on message (offense), thereby pointing people to His Father.

In John chapter 8, when the woman caught in adultery was brought to Jesus, the Jewish religious leaders asked if she should be stoned to death according to the Law of Moses. Again, they were trying to trap Jesus. If He did not uphold the Law, they would have a basis for bringing charges against Him. If He did uphold the letter of the Law, He would likely alienate those to whom He was trying to communicate—the masses. So, instead of directly answering the question, He broadened the terms of the debate in order to uphold the Law, save the woman from stoning and

54

give her an opportunity to leave her life of sin, and put the religious leaders in a defensive posture. His well-known response was, "If any one of you is without sin, let him be the first to throw a stone at her" (John 8:7). The first person to throw a stone would therefore be claiming to be sinless, the same thing to a Jew as claiming equality with God—a crime punishable by stoning. Jesus effectively used his opponents' God-concept to take control of the situation.

In each case, Jesus assumed control of the terms of the debate by ignoring the initial question and then reframing it for His purposes. Much like an able politician or debater, He moved from defense to offense by always redefining the rhetorical playing field, thereby outflanking the opposition. In essence, Jesus hijacked the question. When confronted by those who tried to trap Him, He consistently and skillfully reframed the question so as to stay on message (offense), thereby pointing people to His Father. We should learn how to do likewise, and attempt to do no less.

These examples illustrate the principle of how we can *transcend* almost any issue, including homosexual behavior or abortion, ultimately making the God of the Bible the focus of the debate, allowing us to stay on offense and control the rhetorical playing field.

In today's American culture, we must first recognize that the amoral forces of "tolerance" are currently in the driver's seat, which means those of us who disagree with them are, by default, on the defense. The war in Vietnam painfully reminded us as a nation that a great defense can rarely do more than delay defeat. On the other hand, Bill Clinton demonstrated that the best defense is actually a tireless "take no prisoners" offense. For instance, instead of reacting to the phrase "family values," he hijacked the term by redefining "family" from a father, mother, and children to pretty much whatever the individual wanted it to be. Instead of directly answering questions about Monica Lewinski, he picked a fight over the meaning of "is." Distract. Divert. Spin. Countercharge. He always found a way to duck and then move back onto the offense—to stay on message. Although he lacked any vestige of integrity, he was masterful with rhetoric. Only rarely did he directly answer charges leveled at him. He understood the well-worn political adage, "I don't want my opponent to admit anything; I just want him to deny it." In other words, Bill Clinton understood that in order to win, he had to be on offense making the charges, not trying to defend himself against them. Likewise, our opposition understands that if they can keep us on the defense by controlling the *terms* of the debate, they can also control the outcome. If we are to win, we must reframe the entire issue in a manner that allows us to move back onto the offense—to stay on message.

Therefore, if our rhetorical response is merely to condemn a symptomatic issue such as homosexual behavior, abortion, racism, or pornography as morally reprehensible (which they are), we will lose (i.e., the behavior will continue, or other symptomatic behavior will replace it). In much of our culture, condemning immoral behavior is deemed intolerant (opposition to racism being the one notable exception—at least for now). And if we come across as intolerant, we lose much of our ability to communicate to a large segment of our culture, which is exactly what the opposition wants. But here is the real bottom line: each time we defensively react to their issue, they are able to further marginalize us in the eyes of the broad culture, and worse, get us off message. It is that simple—and that profound.

Matthew 13:24–30 records the story Jesus told of a farmer who discovered that someone had planted weeds in his wheat field. He instructed his employees to let the weeds grow up with the wheat until harvest time, so that uprooting the intertwined weeds would not damage the wheat. Likewise, God does not ask us to pull weeds in His wheat field; rather we are instructed to nurture, water, and fertilize His crop until the time when He harvests it.

In this regard, I believe that when Jesus said, "Do not judge, or you too will be judged," He was making more than just a moral proclamation. He was also making a statement containing the seeds of a powerful strategy, because He knew that the most powerful force in the universe is love, not hate, nor its cousin, condemnation. In the words of Martin Luther King, Jr., "Darkness cannot drive out darkness; only light can do that. Hate cannot drive out hate; only love can do that."[22] Jesus demonstrated this when He laid down His life for us out of love; He did not come to condemn us, even though the basis for condemnation is very real. Therefore, God Himself, the author of love, is the logical starting point in changing our culture.

In order to make God the starting point, we must first establish a clear link in the minds of our fellow citizens between their view of God and their position on any given moral issue. Let me reemphasize that I am not talking about addressing moral content, which comes later in the process. Rather, the goal is to reestablish the critical connection in people's minds between God and morality. In the minds of many Americans, there is a disconnect (a firewall) between belief in God and their position on many moral issues, due to the pervasive influence of moral relativism. This reality is clearly reflected in the question, "How do you *feel* about that?" Whenever we hear this question in regard to a moral issue we should always respond with, "How do you think God feels about that?" We must help reconnect the intellectual disconnect. In this process, the opposition could become one of our greatest allies, albeit unintentionally, similar to what occurred at the University of Washington.

The operating premise here is summed up in the often-heard political response, "That's a good question, but I think the real issue is..." In other words, do not answer the question asked; rather, view the question as an opportunity to talk about our issue—the God of the Bible. As we saw earlier in this chapter, Jesus effectively used this strategy to His advantage on many occasions. Initially, we must strategically ignore the "good question" of the moral rightness or wrongness of a given matter and move immediately to the "critical question" of the existence and identity of God, who is the basis of morality itself. Without God, morality is little more than a fairy tale, an opinion without basis in fact or reality, a suggestion that no one is obligated to embrace, a concept on the same level as Santa Claus and the Easter Bunny.

This tactic is critical for several reasons:

First, the time is ripe. On September 11, 2001, the entire playing field shifted in our favor. Since that day, God has been far more welcome in the public square than He has been in decades. In addition, President George W. Bush and U.S. Senator Joseph Lieberman have already begun the process for us. Bush has been very clear about his personal belief in God, as well as our need as a nation to retain God in the public square. Likewise, Lieberman drew a clear, unambiguous connection between social issues and God in a speech at Notre Dame when he stated, "We as a nation must strengthen our moral foundation because so many of the social problems...are at their heart moral problems." A few moments later he closed the loop by saying, "I believe that we are still struggling to regain our moral balance, in part because we are struggling to regain our spiritual balance."[23]

Second, it allows us to switch the terms of the debate away from issues over which we have limited control, toward an issue that we can frame and direct. The opposition will still attack. In fact, they may initially react with an intensity we rarely see. However, the key difference is that we will be able to begin taking territory rather than continuing to lose it. This does not mean that we will necessarily convince our opponents, but we will be better positioned to influence the thinking of those in the middle who are not already committed to an anti-God ideology.

Third, according to pollster George Barna, 85 percent of Americans consider themselves "Christian," Of these, 8 percent are evangelicals, 33 percent are born-again non-evangelicals, and 44 percent are "notional Christians." (The latter are those who consider themselves to be Christian, but do not embrace core Bible doctrines.)[24] This means we will tend to have an audience predisposed to our point of view. Our challenge is to always relate the debate back to the God of the Bible.

This tactic enables us to make the existence and identity of God the central issue we must debate as a nation.

Fourth, once we establish linkage in people's minds between God and a given moral issue, it will be an easy matter to establish the same link between God and all other moral issues. Once our foot is in the door, it is easy to begin opening it even wider.

Fifth, it enables us to make the existence and identity of God the central issue we must debate as a nation. Once this occurs, we are in the driver's seat. At that point the principles of social change will work in our favor *if we stay on message*. We have the opportunity to shift the debate from sexual preference, death with dignity, or "choice" to the underlying question, "Who is God?"

Sixth, God is the underlying watershed issue.

Let me once again reemphasize, our view of God will determine our belief system as individuals and as a society. If we fail to make the God of the Bible the issue, we shall most certainly and inevitably fail. Not only is God the watershed issue, but "God" is the only issue (when properly framed) that can consistently enable us to maintain control of the rhetorical playing field. Is it therefore any wonder that the opposition strives with such passion to censor religious speech in the public square—especially in education?

Review Questions

1. How comfortable are you in the "offensive" role—taking the debate to our opponents rather than just defending yourself against the opponents' charges?

2. How can Christians balance aggressiveness and love? Are the two compatible or mutually exclusive? When does aggressiveness cross the line of being unloving? Why?

3. How would you evaluate your temperament—pro-active (offense) or compliant (defense)? If you are not naturally aggressive, how willing are you to take on that role when necessary in order to make God the issue?

4. When Jesus demonstrated aggressive behavior in words and action (such as driving the money-changers out of the temple), was He doing something unique to Himself or setting an example for all of His followers? Why?

5. Statistically speaking, why should it not be difficult to reframe the rhetorical debate about God in America with the general population? If the majority of Americans claim to believe in God, why isn't God found throughout the public square in our culture?

CHAPTER 4

Defining Seven Rules of Social Change

"A wise man has great power, and a man of knowledge increases strength."
KING SOLOMON (PROVERBS 24:5)

Any substantive change in society comes with a price tag. Societies, like the people who compose them, resist change, and often make agents of change pay dearly for disrupting the status quo. However, there are some historical rules of engagement that if properly understood and followed will exponentially increase our chances of changing the culture. We can ignore them, but only to the detriment of our cause. Many of them are common sense; others do not seem to be quite so common. Some of them we have already discussed, but the goal of this chapter is to place them in context to show how they work together. Understanding and applying these principles can produce powerful change. As the familiar saying goes, knowledge is power.

RULE #1: A highly committed handful of individuals is required to drive the process of social change.
Only a relative handful of people is required to move the thinking of the broader culture if that group is highly committed to its cause. But they must be willing to sacrifice everything if the need arises. This seems to be what the history books indicate.

Our Founding Fathers understood this principle. All fifty-six of the men who signed the Declaration of Independence knew that they might well die a traitor's death. Nine of their rank did die during the Revolutionary War. Five others were captured and tortured by the British. Twelve lost their homes; seventeen lost their fortunes; two lost their sons. Despite all this, not a single one defected. Not a single man failed to honor his pledge as stated in the final sentence of the Declaration of Independence: "For the support of this declaration, with a firm reliance on the protection of Divine Providence, we mutually pledge to each other our lives, our fortunes, and our sacred honor." In the end, despite the odds, they triumphed.

In 1903, at a meeting of the Russian Social Democratic Labor Party, the qualifications for membership were debated. One man, Vladimir Lenin, vehemently demanded nothing less than total and complete commitment to the Communist cause for life. Seventeen men joined with him. Fourteen years later, when they seized power in the Soviet Union —a nation of 150 million people—there were still only four thousand members of the Communist Party. A handful of people took over one of the most powerful nations on earth, and then proceeded to spread their humanist ideology to the rest of the world through propaganda and military force.[25]

William Wilberforce, a member of the House of Parliament around the turn of the 19th century, persisted for twenty years before seeing the slave trade ended in the British Empire. A small group of influential men known as the Clapham Sect did their part in assisting him. During most of those years his peers in Parliament mercilessly ridiculed him. But in the end he triumphed, standing on the shoulders of the members of the Clapham Sect who had joined with him heart and soul.

Twenty years ago, a young Christian couple decided to tell the people of their nation about Jesus Christ. They were from an Asian country that was closed to the message of God's Son, where any type of proselytizing would result in imprisonment or death. At that time there were approximately five hundred known Christians in the country. Today, the gospel of Jesus Christ has been heard throughout that country as a result of the persistence and tenacity of that one couple who wholly committed themselves to Jesus Christ (enduring imprisonment along the way). As a result, approximately twenty-five percent of that nation's citizens now follow the God of the Bible. And although there are still very real challenges for those who truly follow Jesus, the official policy of that government has changed to one of religious toleration. That nation has forever been changed, and is continuing to change because of two people who were willing to pay the ultimate price if necessary.

All but one of Jesus' disciples died as martyrs (excluding Judas the traitor, of course). The other, John, was tortured by the Romans and then exiled to the island of Patmos. The apostle Paul received thirty-nine lashes on five occasions. He was beaten with rods three times, stoned once, and shipwrecked three times (2 Corinthians 11:23–28). But he, as well as all the other apostles, persevered through overwhelming obstacles. Empowered by the Spirit of God, they turned the Roman Empire upside down.

That is the first principle of social change. There must be a handful who are willing to give everything for the cause—who are willing to persevere no matter the personal cost.

RULE #2: Determine your core agenda and message and make *all* decisions in light of it.

During Bill Clinton's administration I routinely heard that "Bill Clinton's only goal is Bill Clinton." Baloney! He may well have had a massive ego, but he also had a very definite agenda. It was an object that dwarfed everything he gave away in payment.

Had he not had a fatal character flaw when it came to personal integrity and sexual conduct, he probably would have accomplished his goal. Although he beat the Republicans over "Monicagate" (he was impeached but not removed from office), he had to spend so much personal political capital in that battle that he never fully recovered. He became the laughingstock of all Americans—conservatives, moderates, and even many liberals. His sexual conduct became the brunt of jokes on radio and late-night television. It got so bad that Al Gore, while seeking to become the Democratic nominee for President, felt obliged to lay a major televised smooch on his wife during the Democratic National Convention in order to send a clear message to the American people that he was not a philanderer like Clinton. And yet many in the media say that character does not matter in politics today.

There must be a handful who are willing to give everything for the cause—who are willing to persevere no matter the personal cost.

Bill Clinton's agenda was the courts. He wanted to fill the courts with secular revisionist jurists[26] so that America could be reshaped in his image over the next twenty years by circumventing the cantankerous and independently minded legislative process. Legislators are accountable to the people of their districts and states. Judges at the Federal level are largely accountable to no one apart from other judges. Therefore if the courts become stacked with secular revisionist judges, there really is no accountability, and rampant wholesale change can proceed without real impediment.

Needless to say, Clinton did not complete his agenda. Because the Republican-controlled Senate dragged its feet on confirmations, it became clear to Mr. Clinton by the end of his first term in the White House that in order to complete the process he would have to put his hand-picked successor into office in order to finish the job. That man was Al Gore, whose bid for the White House failed by the narrowest margin in history.

The point is this: Bill Clinton had an agenda toward which he moved the nation as far as he could. Anything that did not directly contribute to that agenda was negotiable fodder for building the political capital he needed to push through his primary agenda. Bill Clinton knew what he wanted and made all of his political decisions in light of it. Though we can be thankful he did not accomplish his agenda in full, we can learn from his example the power of making all of our decisions in light of a single goal.

In regard to this principle, allow me a personal reflection for a moment. You read in the Foreword to this book of my father's desire for political activism at the Supreme Court. What you didn't read is that it was more than my mother's guiding hand that kept my father from the activist's role. For nearly half a century my father has constrained himself by choice to follow the path and completing the agenda that God gave Him: fulfilling the Great Commission of Jesus Christ. As badly as he might have wanted to enter other venues, and as capable as he would have been if he had, he stayed focused on his calling and subordinated everything else in life to it. He is a living example of the fruit that is born from setting an agenda and remaining committed to it.

Likewise, we must determine our primary goal and then be willing to give away the rest of the store (if necessary) in order to accomplish it. We cannot win every battle. But if we strategically chose our battles with great care, we can win the war.

RULE #3: Determine your audience.

In determining our audience, two factors are important: the receptivity of a particular audience, and their potential ability to exert influence.

First, the Book of Acts records how the apostle Paul always began his preaching at the local Jewish synagogue whenever he entered a new town. The reason is simple: he was most likely to find a receptive audience there for his message due to the large amount of shared belief. This is generally how Paul got the "camel's nose under the edge of the tent" in a city. Once he had established a base of converts, he could then begin to expand it in any given community— a simple but smart strategy.

At the outset of a political campaign, skilled politicians rarely expend energy trying to "convert" those who are highly committed to another ideology. Instead, they first try to identify, solidify, and energize those who share their beliefs. This fortifies their base. Next, the skilled politician tries to frame a message that would appeal to those who lean in his direction. Finally, he targets those who are not highly committed to either side. These "swing votes" often determine the outcome of the election.

As mentioned in Chapter 3, 85 percent of Americans consider themselves Christian, meaning that up to 85 percent of Americans could be open to our message if we frame it properly. However, we should begin with the evangelical 8 percent (the most logical base for our "God of the Bible" message), expand to the "born-again non-evangelical" 33 percent (those who tend to lean toward accepting our message), then expand to the remaining "notional" 44 percent (those who could go either way). It is a logical progression.

Second, we should try to target centers of influence wherever possible. This can be a geographical place, person, or institution. Paul consistently went to the influential cities of his day—centers of political, economic, religious, and academic influence. This was clearly deliberate on his part. For instance, Athens was an academic center. Ephesus was a religious and economic hub. Corinth was a resort town where many of the "rich and famous" lived. Rome was the political and economic center of the empire (although he went there in chains, he had made it clear that getting there was one of his goals). In Acts 9:15 God told Ananias regarding Paul, "This man is my chosen instrument to carry my name before the Gentiles *and their kings* and before the people of Israel" (emphasis added). Among other things, God specifically tasked Paul with telling the "kings" of his day about Jesus. We should be just as strategic in planning how we may reach the influencers of our day.

It is for this reason that Campus Crusade for Christ often focuses on reaching centers of influence on a campus or in a city, state, or nation. If we reach the influencers, they can help us reach everyone else—either from up front or from behind the scenes. Sometimes influential individuals or groups take a high-profile role. Other times they quietly open doors without much fanfare. Each situation is different, but the principle remains.

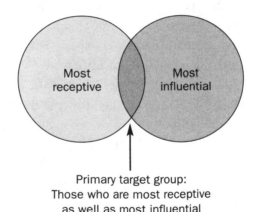

Primary target group:
Those who are most receptive
as well as most influential

In order to succeed, we must be intentional in determining our audience—both those who are most likely to be open to accepting our message and those who can most effectively help us disseminate our message.

71

RULE #4: Tailor your message to your audience.

After we determine our audience, we must tailor our message accordingly. We speak differently to an adult than to a child. My vocabulary when conversing with a philosophy professor is quite different than when I talk with my son's kindergarten teacher. Speaking in a fraternity house is much different than speaking in church on Sunday. Even if the core message is identical, the words are very different—adapted to the particular audience.

The message should be framed from the outset to capture the rhetorical upper hand, often referred to as achieving the "*perceived* moral high ground." It is critical to the process. *If a cause cannot capture the rhetorical offense, it can never win the debate.* This explains in large measure why we continue to lose ground on the issues of abortion ("choice") and homosexual behavior ("tolerance") within the cultural context. If, on the other hand, we can shift the bulk of the debate to discussing who God is, and resist the temptation to go back on the defense by debating cultural symptoms, it will greatly increase our chances of changing the culture itself, despite the inevitable setbacks along the way.

When I was eighteen years old, I traveled with my parents to the former Soviet Union for a couple of weeks. While we were there, our Russian guide told us a joke about a dual track meet between the United States and the Soviet Union, which the Americans won. However, the headline the next day in the Russian newspaper read, "Soviets come in second, Americans next to last." Though fictitious, the story illustrates how perspective (spin) is critical.

The perspective we present affects perception, and perception has power to create change. In politics, many even go so far as to say, "Perception is everything." That is why politicians expend so much energy trying to get just the right "spin." They understand that if you can change a person's perception, then you can also change his beliefs, values, views, and behavior.

About ten years ago while I was in the Philippines, I read in the local newspaper that President Aquino during her trip to the U.S. had met with the Vice President of the United States at a military installation (the article failed to mention which one). The paper was very critical of her for this, because at the time many Filipino activists were trying to oust the U.S. from its military bases in the Philippines. Upon reading the article, I started chuckling. I happened to know which military installation was being referenced—the U.S. Naval Observatory, on the grounds of which is the official residence of the Vice President of the United States. Context does make a difference.

About a year after I joined the staff of Campus Crusade for Christ, I moved to Seattle to work on our ministry team at the University of Washington. Several times people said to me with sympathy in their voice that the Northwest was the most "unchurched" part of the country. The clear implication was that the people there were unresponsive to the gospel. How wrong they were. I soon realized that students in the Northwest were very open to the gospel, but I also quickly learned that I could not use "church" words and had to adapt my presentation accordingly.

In the seven years I was there I spoke to many fraternity pledge classes. With only two exceptions, every time I spoke, over half of the young men present indicated that they would like to know more about how to know God personally. In framing my message, I always began with their felt need and then used that as a springboard into their real need (a relationship with God). For instance, I would go in to talk about "Leadership" and then transition to the greatest Leader who ever lived—Jesus Christ. Or I would talk about "Brotherhood," and then introduce them to the one Person who best modeled what a true brother was—Jesus Christ. The point was always to show in a positive way why the God of the Bible was relevant to their lives today. I was a messenger attempting to deliver the message to the best of my ability, and therefore I worked hard to tailor it to my audience.

> *I quickly learned that I could not use "church" words and had to adapt my presentation accordingly.*

One of the international ministries of Campus Crusade for Christ is called "Crossroads." It uses the issue of AIDS to bring the message of Jesus Christ to people in countries devastated by the epidemic. It is a program designed for schools to use in educating young people about AIDS and how they can protect themselves by changing their behavior. In the process, we present Jesus as the one who can give them the power to make these behavioral changes in their lives. We start from their felt need (avoiding AIDS) and show how it relates to their real everyday need for God.

Jesus did this with great consistency as well. He almost always began with stories to which His audience could relate. He gave them something they could readily understand, and then rhetorically moved them to where He wanted them to go. Most of Jesus' teaching followed this pattern. He not only knew His message—He knew His audience.

With the woman at the well, He spoke first of water (John 4:4–42). With the hated tax collector, He first granted social acceptance by welcoming the opportunity to dine with him (Luke 19:2). With the theologian Nicodemus, He raised the most profound theological issue: "You must be born again" (John 3:1–21). With the woman caught in adultery, He first provided for her physical security by shaming her accusers into leaving (John 8:3–11). Jesus always tailored His words to His audience.

When Paul was in Athens, he framed the message to his audience in a unique way. He saw an altar to "An Unknown God," and used this as the starting point of his speech to the Areopagus—the leading thinkers of the city. He employed it as a springboard into talking about the God who created the universe (Acts 17:16–34).

Someone has said God is like an elevator operator: He meets you at your level and takes you where you need to go.

Recently, I met with several religious leaders of a Christian denomination. They were trying to write a document justifying the actions they were taking in a certain city where they had received a great deal of negative feedback. However, they were trying to write the document to reach both the churched and unchurched at the same time—a truly impossible task. The initial document looked like it was written for theologians, full of "church" language. Had they published it in that form they would have been "tarred and feathered" in the secular press—and it would have been their own fault. Fortunately, after further discussion, they wisely gave it to a writing committee that had a good understanding of how to communicate with a secular audience. The final document was outwardly quite different than the original, even though it basically said the same thing.

George W. Bush, in his response to the Muslim terrorists, said that we would pursue an aggressive "crusade" against them. To the average American, the word is rather innocuous. But to an Arab Muslim whose ancestors were the focus of the "Crusades" almost a thousand years ago, it is just as offensive (even more so, if that is possible) as derogatory racial slurs and epithets are to ethnic minorities in America. To an Arab Muslim, pouring gasoline on a fire is no less inflammatory. Fortunately, President Bush learned quickly and made that mistake only once. Had he done it again, even our closest allies in the Arab world might not have stood with us. The words we use will determine how our audience responds.

In order for our message to be understood, we must understand who our listeners are, how they think, and how they speak. In this regard, *how* we say something is almost as important as *what* we say. As I mentioned in Chapter 2, words like "grace," "salvation," "born again," "sinner," and even "Christian" are often misunderstood by a secular audience. Although these words are very important to all followers of Jesus, our goal should always be to communicate the concepts that the words represent. There is no magic in the words themselves. When missionaries translate the Bible into another language, they must find words and phrases in that language to communicate biblical concepts. We should adopt a similar cross-cultural mindset. Although we must never compromise our message, we desperately need to become experts at communicating the gospel using words our audience understands.

RULE #5: Stay on message. Never react—always reframe!
Following one of our rhetorical skirmishes at the University of Washington, my wife received a plaque from some friends. It had a picture of a skier slicing through the water kicking up a wall of spray. The picture was entitled, "Sometimes, in order to stay the course, you have to make waves." I often think of that picture when I am tempted to throw in the towel and take the route of least resistance.

Staying on message, staying the course, requires being intentional. It takes work, thought, and training. And often it takes courage. But it never "just happens."

If someone approaches you and says, "I'm offended that you prayed in the name of Jesus," your first natural response might be to apologize for having given offense. However, if you have given it thought ahead of time you might respond in the following manner: "I understand what you are saying, but I would encourage you to rethink your position. It sounds like you are promoting censorship rather than open and honest dialogue. I don't really think you want people to regard you that way, do you? And besides, what do you have against Jesus?" In a few short moments, you have put your prosecutor in a defensive position, and you are now back on message, in control of the rhetorical playing field, talking about God. This is exactly what the apostles did routinely, such as when Peter responded to the Sanhedrin's intimidating threats by saying, "Judge for yourselves whether it is right in God's sight to obey you rather than God" (Acts 4:19). Unlike us, it never even seemed to cross their minds to apologize for making Jesus the issue.

If we cannot stay on the offense, we cannot win. A great defense, though important, will not move us forward. The entire process can be summed up in four words: Never react —always reframe! Never, never, never answer the question unless it allows you to go where you want to go!

As I illustrated in Chapter 3, Jesus did this routinely. He never accepted His opponent's terms of debate. He always reframed the issue to make *His* point. Once we allow the opposition to frame the question, we are on the defense. In order to move back onto offense, we must reframe the entire question; we must redefine the rhetorical playing field.

On one university campus in the South, a Christian group ran a set of four ads in the student newspaper featuring former homosexuals. Each ad told an individual's story about how he or she became involved in homosexual behavior. Then the individuals related how a personal relationship with Jesus Christ had so radically changed who they were that they no longer craved the homosexual experience. This of course created an uproar in the homosexual community on that campus. Unfortunately, the leader of the Christian group was inadequately trained to effectively control the controversy. He publicly apologized a few days later for running the ads, instead of turning the tables and legitimately accusing their attackers of hypocrisy and of censoring the speech of people whose experience happened to be different from their own. They therefore allowed the homosexual community to hijack the agenda, making the issue "homophobia" rather than Jesus Christ.

Recently, a politician in Florida who is known to be an honorable Christian man found himself confronted by four homosexual students from a local high school. They demanded to know whether or not he would support their homosexual agenda. Of course, it was a classic set up. He played right into their hands by stating that because the Bible says that homosexual behavior is a sin, he could not support them. For the next few weeks he had to endure a major assault by the local media. By failing to reframe the question that day, he set himself up for inevitable, unavoidable defeat—even though what he said was true.

He could have easily offered to champion their cause for them if they would first do one thing for him—prove beyond a reasonable doubt that the God of the Bible does not exist by disproving the resurrection of Jesus Christ using the historical/legal method of proof (which of course is impossible due to the overwhelming historical evidence for the resurrection).[27] This would have allowed him to get right back on message—making God, not behavior, the issue—while simultaneously turning the tables and putting the four students in a rhetorically defensive posture. He would have still taken shots from the media for this response, but at least it would have moved him away from a rhetorical battle over homosexual behavior, which is very difficult to win in a relativistic culture, to a dialogue about God that he could largely control. Again, the goal is to use the platform to make God the issue.

Alternatively, he could have asked them if they would first be willing to co-sponsor, along with the Christian students, a debate on morality itself and its rational basis since that seems to be the underlying point of disagreement. If they refused, he could have easily questioned their intellectual integrity and their sense of fair play. The point is to always to stay on offense and to advance the God agenda in one way or another.

Jesus never failed to speak the truth, but He always wisely reframed the question in order to present the truth in the best light possible. As long as we continue to accept the opposition's terms of debate, there is little hope of ever winning this battle.

Jesus never failed to speak the truth, but He always wisely reframed the question in order to present the truth in the best light possible.

In his book *Rules for Radicals*, Saul Alinsky, the highly effective political organizer, shrewdly observed, "The real action is in the enemy's reaction...The enemy properly goaded and guided in his reaction will be your major strength."[28] Again, this is using the concept, "I don't want to get my opponent to admit anything; I just want to get him to deny it." The point is to force one's opponent into a reactionary defensive mode. We must always stay on message, and we must force the opposition to react to our agenda if we wish to win.

When we stayed on message at the University of Washington, the high-profile opposition eventually evaporated in discouragement. When William Wilberforce stuck to *his* guns for twenty years, he finally saw the slave trade outlawed.

Because Vladimir Lenin and his associates were totally committed to hammering *their* message home, they took over one of the largest nations on earth. Because the apostle Paul and his associates preached *their* message without deviation despite intense opposition and martyrdom, the course of history was changed.

When we are willing to carefully craft our words and then stay on message no matter the cost, we too can win. But it requires focus, wisdom, a disciplined tongue, and perseverance. Never, never, never feel obligated to answer the question! It can all be summed up in four words: Never react—always reframe!

RULE #6: Eat the elephant one bite at a time.
There is a timeless riddle that asks, "How do you eat an elephant?" The answer: "One bite at a time."

George W. Bush understands the meaning of this adage. A few months after being elected President, he publicly announced that he intended to open up the oil fields in Alaska and off the coasts of California and Florida. This was tantamount to declaring war on the environmental movement—and he knew it. He threw down the glove. Did he really expect to get everything he wanted then and there? Of course not! At the end of the day, what did he do? He "settled" for opening up 1.5 million acres off the coast of Florida for drilling—progress in the direction he wanted to go. His goal was to advance his agenda, which he did. At some point he will revisit the issue, and at the end of the day he will once again appear conciliatory and "settle" for just one more bite out of the elephant. He will again advance his agenda. If he remains persistent in this pursuit, he will eventually eat a lot of that elephant—maybe all of it.

Here is what George W. Bush understands. He knows that effective politics (as well as much of life) is the art of incremental change. It is *not* the art of compromise. The goal is to always advance the agenda, to continually wear the opponent down. At each step, take what you can get and then move to the next step and repeat the process. According to an old Chinese proverb, "The person who removes a mountain begins by carrying away small stones."

The process of incremental change is also much like investing money. If I have a $1,000 and I want to turn it into $1 million, I can invest all of it in the lottery or a get-rich-quick scheme, or I can develop a thirty-year investment strategy that is designed to get me to my goal—incrementally. Which is the wiser approach?

If we wish to see real change, we must understand that it will be incremental. Americans want everything yesterday; even Christians in our culture have not been immune to this malady. We hate "compromise" with the world, and that is good. However, confusing incremental change with compromise is deadly to the advancement of a cause. Apart from the direct intervention of the Spirit of God, we will not see things change overnight in our culture. That is a given.

Demanding all or nothing *today* is much like playing the lottery. It is not a wise strategy and it is highly unlikely to produce any of the results we desire. History itself teaches us this. Although we sometimes perceive dramatic, sweeping change, we must realize that we are seeing only the tip of the iceberg. Real change almost always occurs incrementally on the shoulders of individuals who have often labored in relative obscurity and hardship over an extended period of time. The "dramatic, sweeping change" we occasionally see is merely the highly visible culmination of that process.

For instance, the election of Ronald Reagan brought dramatic changes, not only to America, but to the world as well. He seemed to appear on the scene like an unstoppable juggernaut. And yet, the watershed event that led to Reagan's election in 1980 occurred in 1964 with the defeat of Barry Goldwater. If Goldwater had not run for President, it is highly unlikely that Reagan could have been elected sixteen years later. Goldwater energized conservatives. Many, like Donald Hodel, who became Reagan's Secretary of Interior, stayed involved and ultimately set the stage for Reagan's victory.

Again, we often hear about how William Wilberforce, a member of the British Parliament, brought about the end of the slave trade in the British Empire in the early 1800s. It cost him twenty years of dogged persistence in the face of intense ridicule—even getting laughed off the floor of the Parliament by his peers. Victory, when it finally came, was dramatic, but it did not come cheaply or quickly.

Many baby steps over time lead to victory. If we are going to engage in the battle to restore God to His proper place in society, thereby restoring society itself, may we always choose to be tortoises, not hares. If we want to eat the entire elephant, we had better be prepared to do a lot of chewing for a long time to come. There is no substitute for perseverance. It is what births "dramatic change." It is what will birth a moral, God-centered society.

RULE #7: Embrace opposition.
Opposition is absolutely critical to long-term success. If we articulate a message contrary to the status quo and experience no opposition, we can reasonably conclude that our message was not heard. However, having said that, a negative reaction from the opposition does not necessarily mean that our message was heard and understood. It may be that our message was misunderstood, and that the negative reaction was to a message we did not at all intend.

For example, if we are strident in presenting our message, people may react to us and never even hear the message. Or, we may talk about the necessity of being "born again," but our secular audience hears only that they must *behave* in a specified manner due to the cultural baggage associated with the term. As I stated earlier, when George W. Bush used the term "crusade," he communicated something entirely different to Muslim Arabs than what he intended. We must be wise in how we present our message to a secular audience.

However, if we properly present our message in terms that the culture can understand and still meet with resistance, we should be encouraged. In this case, opposition is a good indicator that our message is getting through. The apostle Paul was often vigorously opposed precisely because his message was getting through—just as he intended.

If we present our message in terms that the culture can understand and still meet with resistance, we should be encouraged.

In light of the foregoing, I am reminded of an adage from the political arena: "The only bad press is no press at all." Although that statement is not entirely true, there is a lot of wisdom in it. A sure-fire way to lose is to allow our cause to be ignored. Even bad press is therefore better than no press, because it helps to raise the profile of our cause. In this sense, controversy is actually our friend. If the opposition and media ignore us, our cause will die a premature death. Active opposition is critical to our long-term success. A reminder: if we control the rhetorical playing field, the opposition must necessarily react to our message. And as long as they are reacting to *our* message, they cannot win.

From time to time I have asked people whether or not they thought former U.S. Congressman Newt Gingrich was successful. I often get the response, "No! Nobody liked him." But then I ask, "What was his primary goal, and did he accomplish it?" Once the question is reframed in that manner, people begin to understand the difference between popularity and success. He created controversy through his "Contract with America," forcing the opposition to react. He then used the high-profile controversy as a platform to get his message out. Personal popularity had little to do with his strategies or actions. Popularity is nice and it can be helpful. But popularity is not the same as, nor necessarily essential to, success.

Consider Martin Luther King, Jr. Was he popular in the overarching culture (especially early on in his role as a civil rights activist)? Outside of the black community, he was considered a great nuisance by a majority of the dominant white culture, particularly in the South. In fact, he was such an annoyance that someone felt it necessary to murder him in cold blood. While he was not very popular outside of the black community, he was immensely successful at moving his cause forward. In retrospect, he has become more popular since his death as his success in advancing the civil rights agenda has been recognized more widely.

Remember Jack Kevorkian, nicknamed "Dr. Death"? When he first came on the scene, the American public reacted negatively because he was promoting active euthanasia (intentional killing of patients). However, it did not take long until he was front and center on our television screens at night, and people were debating the pros and cons of what he was advocating. Even if people did not agree with him, they became engaged in the debate that *he* had framed. As a result, Dr. Kevorkian steadily advanced his agenda with the general public even though he was and is a lightning rod for differing ethical views.

Finally, consider the apostle Paul. Was he well liked, generally speaking, by the culture of his day? Was he successful? Few people in the history of the world have been more successful in accomplishing their goal. He and a handful of others turned the Roman world upside down. And yet, if ever there was a human lightning rod, it was Paul. He was stoned. He was beaten. He was flogged. But his opponents only served to amplify a well-framed message. Paul never confused popularity with success—and neither should we.

> *We do know without a doubt that if we do not make the attempt, we shall most certainly never succeed.*

Newt Gingrich got bad press, as did Martin Luther King, Jack Kevorkian, and the apostle Paul. The irony is, bad press can be good if we are able to harness it to help move our cause forward. If we have done our homework ahead of time, whether our press is good or bad, we should be able to advance our cause. Certainly I prefer good press, but I also understand the necessity of "bad" press as a tool for bringing about change.

Change always comes with a price tag. Among those who knew the price and willingly paid it are Moses, Jesus,

Paul, Lenin, George Washington, William Wilberforce, Abraham Lincoln, and Martin Luther King. Like them, we do not know with certainty that we shall overcome (Jesus being the exception), but we do know without a doubt that if we do not make the attempt, we shall most certainly never succeed. History teaches, time and time again, that none who have advanced their cause have done so for free. A willingness to pay a price, coupled with knowledge of the rules of social change, will ensure the likelihood of victory.

Review Questions

1. How willing would you be to become part of a "highly committed handful of individuals" whose goal was to make God the issue in a given area of our culture? What is the highest price you would pay to achieve success?

2. What is your reaction to learning that, with the exception of John, all the original disciples that Jesus commissioned (including Paul) were martyred for attempting to make God the issue in various cultures? Where in our world today do you see this spirit alive in the Christian church?

3. After reviewing the seven rules of social change, which are the most important for you to adopt in your efforts to make an impact in your circle of influence? Why?

4. What is the difference between responding and reacting in either personal or cultural debate?

5. How do opponents of Christianity help to further our message? What opportunities do they give us by opposing our message (if we will only take advantage of them)?

CHAPTER 5

Reframing the Cultural Rhetoric

"The crowds were profoundly impressed by his answers."
MATTHEW 22:33 (TLB)

Words matter. Jesus, of course, knew this and therefore was always careful to speak wisely. If we wish to win the war for the culture, we must heed the words of Jesus to be "as shrewd as snakes and as innocent as doves" (Matthew 10:16).

It is no secret that Christians consistently get "taken to the woodshed" by the secular media on a number of cultural, ethical, social, and spiritual issues. In fact, the negative press is so bad that if I were a young adult today who grew up outside the church, I would probably believe that Christians oppose just about everything including tolerance, diversity, choice, separation of church and state—and maybe even happiness itself.

Now, many of you probably just responded by thinking, *But we do oppose all of those things—except, or course, for happiness.* To which I say you are exactly right. And therein lies the problem. The broad culture *perceives* us as opposing

91

just about everything, which prevents us from effectively communicating. (Keep in mind that perception constitutes reality for most people.) In fact, I think we often perceive ourselves as opposing just about everything, which shows that we are not the ones in control of the cultural rhetorical playing field. We are on defense, not offense. In effect, we have bought into the culture's perception of us! We spend the bulk of our efforts pulling up cultural "tares" rather than tending the wheat. It is now time for us to become "advocates" rather than "obstructionists" in the minds of our fellow countrymen. Instead of always objecting, we must be advocates of diversity, tolerance, free speech, separation of church and state, taking care of the poor, equality, and other areas where we are viewed as obstructionists. It is time for us to quit reacting, and start reframing.

We must learn to aggressively reframe the rhetoric of the opposition, just as Jesus did. By this I mean that we unabashedly seize the opposition's rhetoric and give it additional or new meaning. We co-opt it. We redefine it. In fact, we must become better at redefining the meaning of words than the modern-day revisionists themselves. This does two things. First, it broadens the meaning of their rhetoric to support and carry our message, while simultaneously diluting their original intent (I will flesh this concept out later in this chapter). Such is what happened to the term "family values" under Bill Clinton. (They redefined "family" to be something other than the traditional nuclear family.) It is also what the militant homosexuals have done to the term "diversity." They have broadened it beyond ethnicity and gender to include sexual behavior. They have literally hijacked the civil rights movement! Second, this approach moves the debate onto our playing field ("God is the issue"), thereby enabling us to control the rhetoric. This allows for forward progress instead of continually running into the proverbial "brick wall" because of a reactive mindset, which by its very nature is defensive.

If we truly wish to win, being intellectually right is not enough. We have been right for a long time but we are still losing ground. In this regard, how our fellow citizens perceive our words is just as important as being right. If they misunderstand our message, then being right does our cause absolutely no good.

I believe one of the key components in the communication process is creating "linkage." Let me illustrate: A bumper sticker I routinely see says "Visualize World Peace"—not a bad slogan. But one day I saw another bumper sticker: "Visualize Whirled Peas." To this day, whenever I see the original bumper sticker I always recall its reworded, counterfeit cousin—and chuckle. That is linkage at work. I cannot think of one without thinking of the other.

Another example is the "Darwin" fish symbol, with evolutionary, leg-like appendages, which people stick on the back of their cars to mock the Christian "fish" symbol seen on other vehicles. It is difficult for me to see one symbol now without thinking of the other. This is another example of linkage. (I have even seen a humorous, reactionary, counter-symbol: a large fish symbol swallowing the Darwin symbol. Now that's re-reframing the issue!)

Linkage is a critical step in the reframing process. In the following pages I will illustrate how to create linkages by redefining cultural terminology, which should allow us to co-opt important issues of our day and reframe them to our advantage in the public debate.

Ultimately, creating linkage on various issues could enable us to achieve the *perceived* moral high ground (in addition to the *actual* moral high ground) within the culture. As you read, please keep in mind that I am not addressing legal or legislative strategies—only rhetorical posturing for making God the issue whether in large groups or one on one. The following examples are not intended to be exhaustive, but merely starting points for consideration.

The bottom line is that we must perceptually position ourselves as "advocates" rather than "obstructionists"—thereby enabling us to make the God of the Bible the issue.

Violence in Public Schools

For a long time now, many have used the increasing violence in public schools as a major vehicle for promoting stricter gun control. We can and should unapologetically turn this issue for our cause as well. I think it could become a powerful tool in our rhetorical arsenal, since all parents are concerned about the safety of their children.

Every time violence in public schools makes the front pages of the newspaper, we should unabashedly assert in our spheres of influence that in the public schools today, we Americans pretend that God is irrelevant to education, but then we act shocked when our children behave as if there really is no God. If we want children to behave as though God exists, we must teach them that He does. If they do not believe it, they will not act like it. It is that simple.

The truth is, violence is a symptom of one's beliefs (ultimately one's God-concept), not a symptom of owning a gun. Our children are merely acting out what we have taught them by our silence as a culture about God. I believe this directly relates to why the great American educator, Noah Webster, known as "the Schoolmaster of the Nation," said, "Education is useless without the Bible."[29]

Both the pro-gun and anti-gun lobbies have missed the real point. Arming law-abiding citizens will not prevent another Columbine. Conversely, disarming the citizenry will not prevent it either, as the high school massacre at Erfurt, Germany, on April 26, 2002, so horrifically demonstrated. Expelled student Robert Steinhaeuser gunned down thirteen teachers, two students, and a police officer at his former school.[30] This was the fourth time that a teen in Germany had killed school personnel or other students in a two-and-a-half-year period.[31] And this despite the fact that Germany imposes very strict gun control on its citizens.

In light of the above, it should be relatively easy to make the rhetorical case that Columbine was caused by *censorship of religious speech, not guns,* since one's God-belief will ultimately determine one's behavior. We are attempting to play off of the gun control debate, trying to create linkage in order to inject our content and take control of the rhetoric.

We should be strategically prepared for any schoolhouse tragedy, of which there will undoubtedly be more since we live in a culture without a moral anchor. While emotions are still raw after such incidents and people are asking "Why?" we can make the connection for them. We must unequivocally place the blame for the tragedy where it belongs—at the feet of those who have removed the only sure foundation of morality from education. But we need to do this with great savvy and wisdom.

When the average parent in America comes to sincerely believe that the safety of his or her own children are at serious risk if God is not a part of education, then the opposition will be hard put to exclude "God" from the schools. Fear for oneself is a powerful emotion, but not as powerful as a mother's fear for her children when their safety is at stake.

Hate Crimes

When the opposition talks about hate crimes, we should talk about *hate crimes against people of faith* such as occurred at

Columbine High School.[32] The "people of faith" addition broadens the rhetoric well beyond what the opposition will deem acceptable. We will link "people of faith" to "hate crimes." Ultimately, the only way they will be able to combat us on this point, because of the linkage, will be to completely omit the phrase "hate crimes" or "hate speech" from their rhetoric—which they will not do, at least in the short term.

Although "hate crimes" legislation includes hate crimes against *people of faith*, they are rarely the focus of the debate. Every official "hate crimes" panel or committee that is convened should be required to look at hate crimes against *people of faith* as well.

The opposition will tend to react defensively (maybe even overreact), in a desperate but hypocritical attempt to keep God and religion out of the debate. When they do, we may pointedly ask why people of faith should not also enjoy the same Constitutional protections (civil rights) they are requesting for themselves. Why should we discriminate against God-fearing Americans? (Please remember, I am not trying to make the legal case; rather, I am reframing the perceptual case for the everyday public debate and conversation so that God becomes the central focus.)

Additionally, we should all drive home the point whenever we engage in dialogue on this issue that "*Hate crimes are symptoms.*" They are no different from any other crimes in that they are merely symptomatic of a far more serious disease. That disease is the main message of this book: the fact that we have excluded God from the public square as the legitimate source of morality. Our culture—via government, education, and the media—has developed a God-phobia that seeks to ban every mention of God from public life. As a result, there is no rational basis for practicing respect instead of hate. Hate crimes are symptoms of teaching moral relativism, of teaching that people are not morally accountable because there is no necessary moral obligation in the universe. They are symptoms of teaching that human life has no inherent value because we are merely a byproduct of "chance plus time," not the concern of a personal Creator. They are symptoms of failing to teach the only rational basis of moral obligation—God Himself.

We should no longer let anyone talk about hate crimes, whether on television, in the workplace, or in our neighborhoods, without asking *why* it is wrong, and then using that as a springboard to talk about the necessity of an intelligent God who is the logical source of all moral obligation.

Tolerance

Similarly, when those who want to justify their immoral behavior talk about tolerance, we should reframe and broaden the focus of the dialogue to include *tolerance of all speech, including religious speech*. We should wrap ourselves in the perceived mantle of being tolerant of all forms of legitimate speech, while implying that the opposition is "selective" and promotes censorship (which they do). Anyone who claims to be tolerant but seeks to exclude speech with which they disagree is anything but tolerant. In the book *1984*, George Orwell referred to such two-faced talk as "doublespeak."

Within this context, the secularists will likely accuse us of intolerance and censorship when it comes to pornography. We should readily plead guilty to trying to protect the innocence of our children from being harmed—something our opposition does not seem to highly value. (If someone is foolish enough to publicly argue that free speech is more important than protecting our children, then give them all the rope they want to rhetorically hang themselves.) Then, without taking a breath, we bring the question right back to their lack of tolerance and overt censorship of certain forms of religious speech and whether we as Americans believe that such hateful intolerance is acceptable. (Remember, try to move back onto offense as quickly as possible.)

Our culture has developed a God-phobia that seeks to ban every mention of God from public life.

We must all daily redefine tolerance as being synonymous with free speech and then create linkage to religious speech by talking about "tolerance of religious speech." We should never miss the opportunity to link the two. This gives "tolerance" a new, broader meaning for the average uncritically thinking American—"free speech." Our neighbors and coworkers should never again hear the word "tolerance"

99

without automatically thinking of "free speech" and "free religious speech." That is linkage. It also allows us once again to move to the "God" issue since we have now incorporated religious speech.

Diversity

We should promote *ethnic and religious diversity* every chance we get. Like savvy politicians, we should take this issue away from the other side by pouring our meaning into it. By adding the terms "ethnic and religious" every time the word "diversity" comes out of our mouths, we are creating linkage. And we should make sure it comes out of our mouths every day so we can redefine it for the culture around us.

We do this for a number of reasons:

- First, it allows us to potentially co-opt the word "diversity," which our culture has already come to largely accept. The other side has worked hard to mainstream this term. Let's aggressively redefine it, giving it new meaning!

- Second, it allows us to isolate and expose what is primarily a sexually motivated agenda. This will force the opposition to overtly admit (or show) that they really mean "sexual" diversity. So far we have let them piggyback sexual perversity on the back of legitimate diversity.

- Third, it allows us to get out in front on the issue of combating racism, which is not only culturally expedient, but is the right thing to do in the eyes of God.

- Fourth, it allows us to inject religion (and therefore the "God of the Bible") into the diversity debate. Much like the homosexuals have done, we overtly piggyback *our* meaning on the term. Once we have injected religion, it is easy to move to the "God of the Bible" issue.

At worst, our efforts will muddy the rhetorical waters. However, at best, we will successfully co-opt the term "diversity." Most importantly, it gives us back control of the rhetorical playing field, adding another platform from which to talk about the "God of the Bible"—which is always the ultimate goal.

Terrorism

Currently, many among the media elite are attempting to create linkage between theologically conservative Christians and the Islamic fundamentalists/terrorists. We should consistently counter with the charge that a person's view of God will determine how he treats others.

If we believe in a God who says, "Kill the infidel," we will likely hate those who do not believe as we do.

If, like Adolph Hitler, we believe there is no God, then we are not obligated to treat anyone with kindness or tolerance because there is no rational source for moral obligation and absolutes.

But if we believe in a God who says, "Love your enemies, do good to those who hate you" (Luke 6:27), then we will be far more likely to extend kindness and respect wherever possible—and not just to those who happen to agree with us.

In this case, we are not creating linkage. Instead, we are using the linkage that others are trying to create as a platform for our message about God-belief and some of its implications.

Corporate Greed

Enron. Arthur Anderson. MCIWorldCom. For a while, the list seemed to grow daily. I have heard numerous people express their shock and dismay over the way many corporations blatantly lied about their finances to cover up mismanagement and outright greed on the part of executives. I fail to understand why people are shocked.

For the past thirty years, our universities have taught a form of ethics and morality that excludes God—the only rational source of moral obligation. Therefore, we should expect deceitful and self-serving behavior to be the norm, not the exception, whether it is visible to the public or not. If a person does not believe that God will hold him accountable for his actions, why would he act in a moral manner if he does not believe it is in his best self-interest? After all, we live in a "Just do it" culture.

More courses on business ethics might help, but they are an incomplete solution. And greater oversight by the Securities and Exchange Commission is not the ultimate answer either. While onerous penalties might slow down certain expressions of greed, they will not stop it. Those are merely Band-Aids applied to symptoms. Unless top corporate executives become convinced that God holds them morally accountable for their business decisions and actions in the marketplace, we will continue to breed more and more "Enrons" every day.

Education that omits "God" is the primary incubator for corporate lying, cheating, and stealing. The point is to link *education that omits "God"* with unethical and illegal corporate greed. Since people already feel strongly about the evilness of corporate greed, we create linkage between that and purely secular education. If corporate executives do not believe in a God who will one day hold them personally responsible, then they are less likely to act responsibly.

President Theodore Roosevelt clearly understood this dynamic as shown in his ominous warning:

> Progress has brought us both unbounded opportunities and unbridled difficulties. Thus, the measure of our civilization will not be that we have done much, but what we have done with that much. I believe that the next half century will determine if we will advance the cause of Christian civilization or revert to the horrors of brutal paganism. The thought of modern industry in the hands of Christian charity is a dream worth dreaming. The thought of industry in the hands of paganism is a nightmare beyond imagining. The choice between the two is upon us.[33]

Dishonesty in the Media

In an age when lies and deceit seem to be the norm (as illustrated in the preceding section), we should be quick to point out the connection between one's God-concept and one's actions. Whether it is a President of the United States lying on the witness stand, or a reporter lying on the front page of the newspaper, we need to help our fellow citizens see the connection between God and truth. Widespread dishonesty is the result of our cultural view of God.

For instance, during my time in politics in our nation's capital, I would occasionally read an article in the newspaper covering a topic or event with which I was well acquainted. In about half of those articles, I observed factual errors—and that does not include the use of innuendo, omission of key facts, or other rhetorical devises used to distort the reader's perception. How much was the result of shoddy reporting and how much was intentional, I am not in a position to say. But what seems clear (especially in light of the book *Bias* by Bernard Goldberg, a former insider at CBS) is that truth consistently takes a back seat to deadlines, personal agendas, ideologies, and ambitions.

Jayson Blair, a former reporter for the *New York Times*, is a recent example. According to numerous reports, he routinely fabricated and plagiarized facts, stories, and sources for his articles. The *Times* was aware that he had a proclivity to lie and yet still kept him in their employ. Even William

Safire of the *Times* admitted on May 12, 2003, "We had plenty of warning." It is one thing to work with a reporter who makes an "honest mistake." But continuing to trust a known liar to report the truth makes about as much sense as hiring a convicted pedophile to take care of one's children. This, of course, raises the question of how many other reporters working for the *Times* engage in similar behavior. Clearly, truth is not the top priority at the *New York Times*. If it were, Mr. Blair would have been fired the first time he was caught lying. Anything less indicates that the *Times* has more important priorities than reporting the truth.[34]

A fuzzy view of God will eventually lead to a fuzzy view of truth. It is a simple matter of cause and effect.

We should not be surprised by the willingness of the secular media to deliberately distort truth or to be a complicit party in that process. Every poll I have seen over the last twenty years indicates that belief in God within the American press corps is substantially lower than that among the general population. Therefore, we should actually expect truth to be a consistent casualty on the evening news and the front page of the newspaper. After all, a fuzzy view of God will eventually lead to a fuzzy view of truth. It is a simple matter of cause and effect. The two are directly linked.

If we fail to connect the dots for our fellow citizens between personal integrity and one's view of God, then we will miss a great opportunity to point people back toward the God of the Bible who says, "Do not lie."

Abortion

A number of years ago I struck up a conversation with a young woman at an event I was attending. As we talked about God and abortion, I made sure I framed my message so that she could hear and understand my words. Near the end of our conversation she said, "You're one of those *compassionate* pro-lifers, aren't you?" Given her tone, she was clearly implying that she perceived most pro-lifers as devoid of all compassion and human warmth. We must change this perception if we are to turn the battle on this issue, but it is not likely to happen through finger pointing (real or even perceived). Most importantly, we must use the issue to point women who have been personally touched by abortion toward the God of the Bible.

There are two potentially effective approaches we can use on this issue. The first is to aggressively make the case that most Americans believe the Bible is correct when it says that man was created in the image of God—that we all bear His image in our very essence. Therefore, we should be very reticent to destroy that image without just cause.[35] Aborting the image of God should be rare because we choose to make it rare. The linkage is between the words "abortion" and the "image of God" within the context of "choice." Juxtaposing the two images allows us to reframe the issue. Our justification once again is based on God Himself.

The point is to drive home the "image of God" rhetoric into the psyche of each and every American. We want to quickly move as many Americans as possible toward overtly viewing the Bible and the God of the Bible as the most legitimate source of moral authority. (Ultimately, we want them to view the God of the Bible as the sole source of legitimate moral authority.) We can use this issue to help in that process.

We can then casually tag on the thought that although abortion may be a "necessary evil" in some cases, it does not have to be a widespread evil in American society. This last turn of phrase allows us to sound reasonable while planting or reinforcing the thought in the listener's mind that abortion really is an "evil." At the proper time when the culture is ready, we can drop the word "necessary."

For rhetorical purposes, we should generally avoid talking about "legislating" morality; rather, we are simply "promoting" morality and preserving the "image of God." Most Americans would agree that we should "promote" morality. And if we say this nicely, in a non-confrontational way—a compassionate way—the American people should be able to hear our words.

This rhetoric accomplishes two things. First, it allows us to once again show how "God" relates to real-life decisions in a way that the average American can hear. We all like to hear that we have intrinsic worth in God's eyes. That is a very positive message that we should all attempt to emphasize whenever possible. In addition, 85 percent of Americans say they believe in the "God of the Bible," so we simply link the two beliefs by stating the Bible says that man was created in the image of God. This may well give us the ability to move people's thinking on the issue itself, because of the likely conclusion they themselves will reach over time. But most importantly, it allows us to once again posit "God" as the focal point.

However, there may be a far more emotionally powerful argument that can be made. The plague of abortion has sewn the seeds of its own demise. There are a great many women —quite possibly numbering in the millions—who are still suffering emotionally (including recurring nightmares) because of abortions they had when they were younger. Strategically highlighting their personal experiences in the context of the forgiveness only God can provide can have two very tangible effects.

First, it would allow us to reach out to those women who are hurting emotionally as the result of an abortion, offering them God's love, forgiveness, and healing.

Second, if properly framed, it could move us as a culture well down the path to making abortions "rare" through young women exercising their "choice" not to have an abortion. We now live in a culture where emotional arguments hold more weight than intellectual ones. Pain is a powerful emotional argument. When confronted with the reality of the potential emotional pain that abortion can bring, many young women may well decide, of their own accord, to avoid such pain.

But most importantly, in this process, many wounded women (both those who have had abortions and those who are considering one) may finally find the love and forgiveness for which they are so desperately looking. Extending love (and being perceived as extending love) rather than condemnation is the model God has given us in Jesus Christ. In essence we link their pain (or potential pain) to abortion, while linking emotional healing to God.

The people who need to lead in the process are the women who have been personally wounded by this harmful plague but have since experienced God's overwhelming love, forgiveness, and healing. The rest of us need to do everything we can to actively support them—through prayer, unconditional acceptance, finances, administrative support, and continual words of encouragement.

Homosexual Behavior

This is the toughest issue we are going to face over the next decade. The other side is well organized and has refined their message and the machinery to deliver it.

A year ago I sat down behind closed doors with a leading national political figure who is a follower of Jesus Christ. With pain on his face, he said that the last time he spoke up criticizing homosexual behavior, he got hammered in the news media every single day for the following six months. I have not heard him say anything about homosexual behavior recently. And he is not unique in his experience among Christians operating in the political arena.

Not long ago I had lunch with a prominent banker. We began talking about some of the challenges he faces as a Christian in the marketplace. In that context the issue arose of "benefits for domestic partners" (wherein the partners of practicing homosexual employees receive the same corporate benefits as do the married spouses of heterosexual employees). He was straightforward. He said that so far his company had been able to resist, but that it was coming at them "like a freight train."

If we accept the current terms of engagement regarding homosexual behavior in our culture today, we will lose.

If we accept the current terms of engagement regarding homosexual behavior in our culture today, we will lose, just like we lost the battle over abortion. Given our current rhetorical posture, we are going to get run over by it—unless we can reframe it.

Rhetorically, we must stop viewing homosexual behavior primarily as an issue to be confronted and addressed. Pagans are going to act like pagans no matter what we do. Instead, we must begin to view homosexual behavior as a platform from which to discuss God. This will require varied strategies depending upon the setting, but the goal in each case will be to co-opt the issue, not to react to it. In many cases, we must strategically ignore the issue itself. Following are some examples:

- When homosexuals promote their behavior in the classroom, we firmly and *publicly* insist on being able to exercise our free speech rights as well, requesting equal time to talk about the God of the Bible, since many Christian students are harassed and belittled for their faith by peers, teachers, and administrators. In many cases they are even deprived of their right to free speech.

- When homosexuals hold sensitivity training classes in Corporation XYZ, we graciously demand equal opportunity to promote our views—especially with employers who are sympathetic to our cause. If Corporation XYZ does not cooperate, we publicly chastise them (with a reasonable tone in our voice and a warm smile on our face) for actively promoting intolerance toward people of faith.

- When the United Way tries to eliminate funding for the Boy Scouts because they do not allow people who engage in homosexual behavior to be scout leaders, we publicly accuse the United Way of censorship, bigotry, and of being "intolerant" of religious belief (all of which would be true). Then we strongly request that, in order to show that they really are tolerant and sorry for such hateful, anti-religious bigotry, they give money to a designated Christian charity.

- When homosexuals in a high school show up in their state legislator's office demanding assistance, he or she should turn the tables by asking if they will first co-sponsor a debate in their school on morality and the basis of morality, since that seems to be the underlying point of contention. Any reluctance on their part should be highlighted as demonstrating a lack of integrity and fair play, which we should label as intolerance. Christian students on a high school campus could use this strategy to sponsor a debate before the entire student body.[36]

- When secularists introduce hate crime and hate speech legislation, we should attempt to attach amendments to those bills stating that the bill should in no wise be construed to restrict religious speech in any form, manner, or location. When they complain or oppose us we can easily ask them why they want to censor the speech of people of faith. To be successful, we must always keep the other side on the defensive.

The one thing we must never, never, ever do, is allow the debate to become focused on homosexual behavior in such cases. It puts us on the defense. If we want to turn the cultural tide, we must rapidly transition to offense. We cannot stop a freight train barreling down on us, but we can strategically derail or hijack it in order to make God the issue.

Morality

Finally, when secularists talk about morality in any context, we can respond by saying, *"Morality is merely a fairy tale unless a rational God exists—a God like the God of the Bible."* Teaching values apart from God is like explaining how a light bulb works without ever mentioning electricity, or talking about how the automobile runs but never referring to the internal combustion engine. Talking about values and morality is meaningless if divorced from their source. If there is no God, we are simply arguing about conflicting preferences, not right and wrong, not good and evil. Right and wrong cease to exist the moment God is removed from the equation.

To drive the point home, we can quote Adolph Hitler, who purportedly said, "Success is the sole earthly judge of right and wrong." If the God of the Bible does not exist, then what rational basis do we have for condemning Hitler's words and actions? I may "feel" that he was wrong, but that does not make him wrong. All it means is that I feel a certain way. It is a morally non-compelling statement without teeth. And if Hitler were alive today, I certainly doubt he would care about how I "feel."

This gives us the opportunity to point out that *if God does not exist, then Adolph Hitler did not necessarily do anything morally wrong.* Again, we create linkage between one's behavior and one's source of moral belief. We need to be able to rhetorically demonstrate that even *attempting* to teach morality (including "tolerance") without first positing "God" is futile and ridiculous, because morality apart from God is no more than a child's fairy tale. If God does not exist, I am not obligated to act in a moral fashion. Not only are those words true, they are absolutely horrifying when viewed through the eyes of history. This is a message that we must imbed in our rhetoric whenever we discuss moral issues. We must show that behavior follows belief.

At some point someone will likely claim it is a false argument to say that if the God of the Bible does not exist, then we have no basis for condemning Hitler, since there are many other religions in the world from which morality can be learned. The simplest response is to reply, "I believe that if the God of the Bible does not exist, then it is irrational to even believe in God at all. Therefore, if you can prove to me beyond a reasonable doubt that the God of the Bible does not exist, I will change my position on homosexual behavior, pedophilia, abortion, incest, pornography, rape, murder, lying, cheating, stealing, and even genocide." The point is to use the issue to keep the focus on the God of the Bible, not to give other religious beliefs a platform.

Separation of Church and State

We will inevitably be accused of trying to violate the so-called doctrine of "separation of church and state" as we advance the "God" issue. When we are so accused, we should forthrightly seize the phrase as our own in order to redefine it.

(Let me remind the reader that I say this from a rhetorical perspective, not a legal one.) We do ourselves no favors by rowing upstream trying to argue *against* separation of church and state. Whether we like it or not, the average American believes in it. Therefore, they should perceive us as "believing" in it as well. After all, people do not resist their own ideas. We should boldly steal the rhetoric from the opposition and then redefine it just like the anti-God revisionists do to us all the time. And we can do it without compromising our beliefs at all.

We could shrewdly respond that we, along with Thomas Jefferson, *strongly* believe in the separation of church and state. Jefferson believed that the federal government should have no jurisdiction over religion or religious speech. In 1798 he wrote, "No power over the freedom of religion... [is] delegated to the United States by the Constitution."[37]

Thomas Jefferson advocated separation of church and state. However, groups like the American Civil Liberties Union (ACLU) seem to agitate for "*segregation* of church and state." Jefferson believed in freedom *of* religion whereas the ACLU lobbies for freedom *from* religion. Thomas Jefferson's primary concern was to *protect and promote* religious speech, whereas the ACLU pushes the federal government and the courts to *censor* religious speech—especially in education.

Jefferson believed liberty must have a rational basis. The ACLU apparently would argue, "Liberty happens." Portions of the following statement, made by Thomas Jefferson in

1781, are engraved on the Jefferson Memorial in Washington, D.C.: "God who gave us life gave us liberty. And can the liberties of a nation be thought secure when we have removed their only firm basis, a conviction in the minds of the people that these liberties are the Gift of God?"[38]

Thomas Jefferson believed morality needed a solid foundation. The ACLU apparently believes, along with Adolph Hitler, that something other than God "is the sole earthly judge of right and wrong." (I would be fascinated to know what, or who, they think is that ultimate arbiter of good and evil.) In this regard, I strongly suspect that Jefferson himself would agree that *segregation* of church and state was the primary cause of the Columbine massacre, as well as most of the violent behavior in public schools today.

The anti-God opposition has heavily promoted Thomas Jefferson, making him their poster child. It's time we recapture him and make him ours—thereby outflanking the opposition. It's a lot less work than rowing upstream.

The goal is to begin giving the phrase "separation of church and state" a new *perceived* meaning for the average citizen. We do this by first recasting the opposition's use of the term as "segregation of church and state," and then accusing them of censorship of religious speech—which is what they do. Again, the worst-case scenario is that raising the issue of "segregation of church and state" will simply muddy the waters. Given the current perceptual climate, that would be an improvement. However, the best-case scenario is that it will be a one-two punch that will inflict great damage on the opposition. Most importantly, however, it will give us control of the rhetorical playing field in order to more effectively make God the issue.

"Segregation of church and state" is a phrase we need to drive home every chance we get if we wish to reopen arenas that are currently closed or are closing to "God" speech. And it is easy to do. When a teacher mentions separation of church and state, a student can simply reframe it. When a school board member or a principal espouses separation of church and state, a parent can easily turn the issue with this phrase. The potential applications are numerous. This brings to mind the words of the late Rev. E. V. Hill, who pastored Mt. Zion Missionary Baptist Church in Los Angeles: "If you want to make a point, use a sledgehammer." This is one phrase where we should unabashedly employ the E. V. Hill sledgehammer method of communication as often as possible.

I strongly suspect Jefferson would agree that segregation of church and state was the primary cause of the Columbine massacre.

If we can successfully undercut the anti-God opposition by boldly seizing this one phrase, I believe we can leapfrog forward in the war to inject the God of the Bible back into the culture, including public education, thereby reestablishing a rational basis for morality.

There may well be a receptive audience for the use of this phrase. As Democratic U.S. Senator Joseph Lieberman said, "The line between church and state is an important one, and has always been critical for us to draw. But in recent years I fear we've gone far beyond what the framers imagined in separating the two."[39] We need to create a rhetorical environment where we turn the existing perception on its head.

Conclusion

All the preceding examples have one purpose: to demonstrate how we can confront the American culture with the God of the Bible. Through creating linkage wherever possible, or at least using cultural issues as springboards, we give ourselves a platform from which to talk about God in a manner that the culture can understand and potentially embrace.

Our responses should always intentionally move us away from an argument we cannot *perceptually* win within the current cultural context, to a place where we can redefine the perceptual terms of the entire debate. In every scenario, our goal is always to make the God of the Bible the issue. Once God becomes the watershed issue, we can then, and only then, begin to pour substantive content into the debate. Remember the watchword of this strategy: Never react—always reframe.

Review Questions

1. Why does being "right" not ensure success? If we are right about God, yet are not changing our culture, what are we lacking?

2. How would you define the effectiveness of "linkages" in reframing the cultural debate? Which of the examples given in this chapter could you most easily appropriate?

3. Cite an instance when you responded defensively to an opponent of God. How might you have reframed the issue to put your opponent on the defensive and make God the issue? What linkage could you have employed?

4. Why is God the central issue in all discussions regarding cultural ills such as intolerance, hate crimes, racism, and others? How can any discussion about these issues be reframed to make God the focus?

5. How does the manner in which we present God (compassionately vs. arrogantly) make a difference in how our opponents respond to what we say?

CHAPTER 6

Building a New Dike

"The definition of insanity is doing the same thing over and over and expecting different results."
BENJAMIN FRANKLIN

Franklin's wise saying is true. If we continue with the same basic game plan we have been operating under for the past few decades—promoting Judeo-Christian morality and ethics (symptoms) without tying them directly to the Judeo-Christian God (cause)—it is not reasonable to expect that much will change in terms of our culture's moral direction. Morality (symptoms) should not be the end point; rather, it should be a springboard from which to launch our message —God (cause). Likewise, if we continue to present God in a way that most Americans find irrelevant to their lives, our fate will be no better. Well-known economist Barry Asmus wrote a book entitled *When Riding a Dead Horse, for Heaven's Sake…Dismount!*[40] We would be wise to heed his words.

Two years ago, while visiting Amsterdam, my wife and I took a bus tour of the lush Dutch countryside. Along the way we saw many dikes crisscrossing the low-lying land-scape. Much of the country rests below sea level and there-fore maintaining these dikes is critical. Our tour guide relat-ed the familiar fable of the little Dutch boy who held back the waters of the sea all night by keeping his finger in the dike. Had it not been for his sharp eyes and determination, the sea would have breached the dike by morning. Fortu-nately for America, we have had many who have figuratively kept a finger in the dike.

As we drove further, we saw a new dike under construc-tion. They were building it further out into the midst of the sea with the intent of draining land currently underwater. It was clearly a major undertaking. Our guide explained that the Dutch have been reclaiming land from the sea for many generations.

We can learn much from the Dutch example. Maintain-ing the current dikes is critical to their survival as a people, much as it is critical that we attempt to maintain the moral dikes that already exist in our country. However, like the Dutch, we must build a new dike out in the midst of the secular sea in order to thrust back the waters of secular hu-manism. We must build it on the foundations of the origi-nal dike established by the founders of this nation; if rebuilt and maintained, this new dike will serve as a bulwark against the tides of moral relativism. Not only will this move our cause forward, but it will also have the net effect of relieving the mounting pressure on the current dikes—in essence, repelling the tide of immorality that currently assails us.

To see how far the sea of secularism and relativism has encroached upon our nation's moral terrain, consider the following questions. They help identify what the original dike was that our forefathers put in place to ensure a land of spiritual and moral health:

- Why did the Pilgrims and others come to America in the first place?

- What was the lead issue that was addressed by the very first amendment to the Constitution?

- What kind of speech has the secular "intellectual elite" virulently assailed in an overt attempt to drive it from the public square?

- Which came first: court rulings compromising and suppressing religious speech, or rulings legalizing abortion and numerous other cultural evils?

The original dike in the American Experiment was an overriding belief in the God of the Bible. He is *the* issue. The majority of Americans say they believe in the God of the Bible. The problem is that most of those people barely have a clue who He is. As a friend of mine likes to say, "Most Americans believe in the Bible because they do not know what it says." We need to help our fellow citizens rediscover the Bible and the God of the Bible, but we must do it creatively, employing new strategies. The old ones are simply not working. Continuing to focus primarily on shoring up the existing dikes clearly qualifies as an example of "insanity": continuing to do the same thing while expecting different results.

Our challenge is now to figure out how we can make God central to the debate throughout our entire culture, in a manner that can be *intellectually* understood and *emotionally* accepted by the masses. We must create linkage between what Americans already believe and the "God" issue, much as the apostle Paul did in Athens, using the idol to "An Unknown God" to talk about Jesus. After all, people do not resist their own ideas. We simply take their beliefs, co-opt and redefine them, and give them new meaning. Their beliefs are our springboard. *The process is less about "changing" beliefs, and more about pouring new content into existing ones.* Of course, in the real world, the net effect is an actual change in belief.

Like Paul, we must look at everything as an opportunity to teach about who God is in a manner that can be understood by our audience—the American public. We must unapologetically co-opt every conceivable platform in order to reframe the cultural agenda. We must learn to take any word or phrase and give it new meaning, forcing the opposition to react to us, rather than continuing with our typical knee-jerk responses which the secular media so willingly exploits.

Building on Opportunities

In December 2001, Dr. Jack Kevorkian appeared on the CBS program "60 Minutes." They showed footage of him actively euthanizing (intentionally killing) his patient by lethal injection. Dan Rather asked him why he would do this on national television knowing that he would be arrested for it. His answer was very telling. He said that either he would win the court battle, which would make active euthanasia legal, or he would go to prison and starve himself to death, becoming a martyr for the cause. Either way, he figured his cause would win the battle. Dr. Kevorkian did go to prison but then he chickened out. He is still alive. He is not a martyr.

He almost gave the pastors of America a golden opportunity of epic proportions. If he had actually tried to starve himself, his entire platform could have easily been co-opted. Pastors and religious leaders of America could have offered to champion his cause for him if he would do one simple thing—prove to them beyond a reasonable doubt that the God of the Bible does not exist (which would be quite impossible to do). Every pastor could have stood up in his pulpit on Sunday morning and made the offer. Or a well-known Christian leader or pastor could have gone on a show such as "Larry King Live" and made the offer. The possibilities would be numerous.

Of course, the point is to show how one's God-belief (cause) is tied to one's view on euthanasia (symptom). Again, we are seeking to establish linkage. If God does not exist, then we do not need to be concerned that we are destroying His image. However, if He does exist, then we need to carefully consider how and when (if ever) it is okay to destroy that image. Therefore, God, not the symptom of euthanasia, becomes the issue. We could have easily co-opted the platform. In addition, because we would have addressed the issue of the individual being created in the image of God, it would have had a potential spillover effect on other issues such as abortion and racism. I hope we are given many such opportunities in the future. But we must be ready to move when those opportunities come in order to make the "God of the Bible" the issue.

When we remove God from the classroom, why are we shocked when people behave as if there is no God?

Some of the best opportunities are those involving people's emotions—including their fears. This is even more true today than in the past, because most Americans tend to base their beliefs largely on how they feel rather than on what they think (as reflected in the American mantra, "How does that make you feel?").

During my time working in politics in Washington, D.C., I observed that the issues that move the masses the quickest generally relate to crime or their pocketbook. When we could convince people that their safety or security was at stake, public opinion moved very quickly. What I frequently observed was outright manipulation for political gain, often involving half-truths and over-sensationalized examples.

We can use the same basic principle—appealing to people's emotions to catch their attention—as long as we are careful to stay well within the bounds of what is true and honest. When Jonathan Edwards preached his famous sermon "Sinners in the Hands of an Angry God," he did not sensationalize the topic (it is said that he delivered his entire message in a monotone voice). He did not need to do so. He simply stated what was true. But it did scare people and cause them to reconsider where they stood in relationship to God. Ultimately it led to major spiritual revival throughout New England. Likewise, we should become masters of framing the emotional issue so that people will listen to us and embrace our message. Once they have emotionally accepted the basic message about God, we can then pour intellectual content into the belief. But we must ensure we are honest in the process.

When the next Enron scandal hits, we must *all*—from the White House to the schoolhouse—forthrightly state that this was to be expected, and we should expect a lot more because the only firm basis of morality was removed from education. *When we remove God from the classroom, why are we shocked when people behave as if there is no God?* It is merely the logical and necessary outcome. If there is no God, it is not wrong to lie to stockholders or even to steal other people's retirement funds.

When the next terrorist strikes at the heart of America, we should *all* make the obvious point—that our view of God will determine our behavior. Jesus of Nazareth said, "Love your neighbor as yourself," and, "Love your enemies, do good to those who hate you." Then He demonstrated what He meant by dying on a cross for us because He loved us. On the other hand, Mohammed in Surah 9 of the Koran said, "Kill the infidel."[41] Unfortunately, many Muslims have apparently taken his statement to heart. Why else would 73 percent of Lebanese Muslims say that they support suicide bombers (as happened at the World Trade Center)?[42] Why else would over a quarter of the Muslims in ten other nations also support suicide bombings?[43]

When a child once again shoots his fellow students, we must *all* (especially those most directly affected) emphatically point out that this is the logical result of leaving the God of the Bible out of education. If we want children to behave as if there is a God, we must as a culture teach them that there actually is a God. If we do not teach it, they will not believe it. And if they do not believe it, they most certainly will not act like it.

If we address people's fears honestly, we will get their attention. However, simply addressing their fears is not enough. We must also take every opportunity to educate them, as well as reeducate those who have been marginalized by a system that portrays God as irrelevant to real life. We need to do this on the national, state, and local levels simultaneously.

Building on Your Platform

We all have a God-given platform. What is yours? Are you a teacher, a businessman, a "soccer mom," a politician, a construction worker, a musician, or an athlete? Are you black, brown, white, handicapped, male, or female? God has given you a platform. Determine what it is, then figure out how to use it. In the words of President Theodore Roosevelt, "Do what you can with what you have where you are."

Are you a teacher in the public schools? Great! When you are required to teach naturalistic evolution in the classroom, give a balanced and objective presentation, taking every opportunity to candidly point out the logical and scientific problems of the theory. This, of course, will lead to questions from the students regarding viable alternatives. At this point it is perfectly appropriate for you to point out other "reasonable" options. Start by showing how the existence of a "Designer" could resolve the inherent irreconcilable flaws of naturalistic evolution. Seek to further reframe the issue by engaging your students in an ongoing discussion of Intelligent Design (a scientific theory that admits the possibility and necessity of God).[44]

The real point is not to initially argue about whether evolution itself is true or false (that is a separate debate). Rather, the goal is to use the platform to show that God is absolutely necessary to make any explanation of creation plausible. God Himself, not His creation, is the critical issue. The primary reason secularists demand evolution be taught is that they want young people to believe that "God" is an unnecessary element in the equation of the universe. That seems to be the real point of teaching evolution. If it were not for that single issue, evolution would have been abandoned long ago as an unviable theory. When the masses come to believe that even evolution cannot be true unless God exists, then evolution itself will cease to dominate education since it will no longer be an effective tool in the hands of secularists with which to marginalize the culture's God-concept.

Many "purists" will balk at the suggestion that we not immediately argue against evolution. However, even the apostle Paul used an idol in Athens to talk about the God of creation. Instead of condemning idolatry in a knee-jerk fashion as I would often be prone to do, Paul used it as a springboard. His goal was to address the underlying core belief first.

In light of this, we want to intentionally and unabashedly co-opt the platform of evolution and use it to convey *our* message—that God does exist and is the center of all creation and the universe—as Paul did with the idol in Athens. As with other issues, the goal is to pour new content into a widely held cultural belief (in this case, evolution). We can use it to move students in the right direction— toward the Cause. We must always make God Himself *the* issue. Resist the temptation to debate symptoms until you have effectively reframed the larger context. If we show that even the theory of evolution cannot be true apart from God's existence, then we have won the central battle. We must help our culture understand on the most basic emotional level that one's God-belief is critical to every area of life.

During Black History Month, a teacher can highlight the biographies of the leading abolitionists. Most leaders of the abolitionist movement were sincere followers of Jesus Christ and understood that God was deeply grieved by the enslavement of black people in America. Levi Coffin, designated "President of the Underground Railroad," said, "The Bible, in bidding us to feed the hungry and clothe the naked, said nothing about color, and I...try to follow...the teachings of that good book."[45] It was God-fearing people, not secularists, who put everything on the line and led the abolitionist movement to break the God-cursed yoke of slavery in this nation.

When teaching about Nazi Germany, explain that Hitler embraced the teachings of Nietzsche who said that because God does not exist the heroic *Übermensch* (superman) should rise up and create society in his own image. That is exactly what Hitler did. When discussing the former Soviet Union, we should point out that the Stalinists, who rejected the idea of God, murdered 110 million of their own people according to Russian intellectual and dissident Aleksandr Solzhenitsyn.[46] And when covering the Inquisition and the Crusades, point out how a fatally flawed view of God led to such "intolerant" and barbaric behavior on the part of those who claimed the name of Christ but did not follow Him. Jesus said we are to love God with all our heart, love our neighbor, and love our enemies. If those who led the Crusades and the Inquisition had been true followers of Jesus, they could not have ignored His commands. They merely hijacked the prevailing power structures of their day to pursue an anti-Christ agenda under the guise of Christianity. The point is to show that an improper view of God leads to dire results. We must demonstrate in each case (within the historical context) that it is was a flawed view of God that ultimately led to such "hate crimes" against humanity—and ultimately even against God Himself.

Are you a musician? "Salt" your music with creative phrases, stories, innuendo, and emotional word pictures that begin to create cultural linkage to the God of the Bible. Although many are already doing that, music is such a powerful medium that even more are needed—especially those who know how to craft words and sound to evoke an emotional response. Since we no longer live in a rational culture, but an emotive one, this is more important than ever before.

Are you a "soccer mom"? Create an environment in your home that feels warm, fun, and safe—an environment where your children's friends will want to come and hang out. If you are typical, your home is the best (but least utilized) asset that the church has. Make your home the place where every neighborhood child stops by to get a cookie and chat. In the process, begin to graciously expose them in numerous ways to the God of the Bible. At Christmas, prominently display Santa kneeling at the manger. At Easter, hold an Easter Egg hunt and invite parents as well. Send everyone home with a nicely wrapped copy of the children's version of the *JESUS* video or DVD.[47] At Halloween, try to hand out the best treats on the block, and include an evangelistic tract for children. During the summer, hold a Backyard Bible Club in your home for your children's friends. Hold a monthly game night for any of your friends and neighbors who want to come—with no RSVP. Offer to take your children's friends to church with you when appropriate. You do not have to talk about God on every occasion, but always think creatively about how you can ultimately make Him the focus.

Perhaps you are a businessman or woman. Bring in motivational speakers who incorporate a spiritual dimension in their talks.[48] Business owners can provide scholarships for workers who may be having marital problems so they can attend a marriage conference to learn how to build a successful marriage—based on a biblical worldview. They can create an environment where Bible study groups can flourish. They can give to Christian charities, or to organizations like the United Way *with strings attached* regarding where that money may or may not be given. Many owners can intentionally create a platform for themselves by being the pitchman for their own product on television (the late Dave Thomas of Wendy's did this very well). By raising their own profile, they can have greater influence not just economically, but for God's agenda as well. Business owners can also run commercials and advertisements in many forms that tactfully weave in the God of the Bible. The possibilities are almost endless.

Are you a golfer? A friend of mine plays a lot of golf and hosts many a foursome at his golf club. Before teeing off at the first hole, he leads the other men in a *very brief* non-threatening prayer thanking God for the beautiful weather and His creation that they get to enjoy. That has opened the door for many natural conversations about God over the ensuing four hours.

Sometimes we become so focused on teaching correct doctrine that we inadvertently deemphasize God and His character.

Are you a politician? You can use your platform to point people to the God of the Bible. Instead of reacting against homosexual behavior (or abortion, etc.), simply reframe the issue. A politician with principle is going to take heat anyway, so he or she may as well maximize the opportunity by saying, "Homosexual behavior is a symptom of what one believes to be true about God. Therefore the real debate we must hold as a culture is who we believe God to be. Until we decide the underlying issue, we will never reach consensus on the symptom of homosexual behavior." Of course, this will create a reaction, which is fine because we now have the debate on our playing field, and we have created linkage in the minds of the audience that over time can be broadened to other issues as well. Additionally, in many cases it may prompt the question, "What do you believe about God?" at which point a savvy politician can quickly and graciously relate his or her own personal spiritual journey—a highly effective way to both control the playing field and communicate with today's feelings-oriented culture.

Building on Our Base

Followers of Jesus still largely own one institution within American society—the church. It is our base. Although it is being attacked from the inside as well as the outside, it remains a potentially powerful force for reshaping the cultural view of God. But we must think strategically how to best employ it and its resources.

When a person desires to become a member of a local church, we should seek to ensure a biblical understanding of who God really is.[49](Sometimes we become so focused on teaching correct doctrine that we inadvertently deemphasize God and His character.) This is a wide-open opportunity for every pastor to reeducate the people coming into his church, greatly increasing the possibility that they will become an others-centered asset rather than a self-centered liability. But in order to do this, we must help them discover who the God of the Bible really is, because their God-belief will ultimately determine their behavior and their ability to be others-centered. Good doctrine is important, but a correct God-concept is absolutely critical.

Second, the church still "owns" the institution of marriage in this country. Most young people want to be married in a church, and 82 percent of American teens indicate a very strong desire to be married to only one person for a lifetime.[50] When a young couple asks a pastor to marry them, he should take the opportunity to help them set a firm foundation for their marriage by ensuring that they understand who God really is (not who the pop culture feels He is). They should be taught God's view of marriage based upon His attributes so that the two are inextricably linked. This can easily be done in a small-group setting. This is an opportunity the local pastor can leverage in order to reeducate young people who have been indoctrinated for years by a system that taught them how to live without God.[51] We want to retrain them. But let me reemphasize, the goal is not just to teach them a biblical view of marriage, but more importantly to teach them a biblical view of God. If we teach them a biblical view of marriage (symptom) without tying it to a biblical view of God (cause), underlying problems still remain and will inevitably surface in the future. We must help them discover who God really is. God Himself is the anchor.

Third, when a young couple starts a family, where do they often go (as least initially)? They check out their local church. If it meets their *felt* needs (such as a quality nursery, children's programs, camaraderie, and encouragement), they are more likely to stay. Again, we can use the felt need as a vehicle for addressing the real underlying need. Think of it as a Trojan Horse process. We give them what they want (a great place for their kids), but then we use that to also give them what they need (an accurate view of God). In many cases the children will become the virtual gateway for delivering the real message to the parents, especially if we are intentional about reconstructing their God-concept with tangible applications.

Fourth, when children walk through the door of our church, we should help them understand who God is. By teaching them God's attributes and character, and training them to walk with God, we can help inoculate them from the messages with which the culture is going to bombard them. It will give them an absolute standard by which to measure everything. Adolescence is where we begin to lose them as they encounter moral relativism in the classroom and the media. At that point we need to actively train them how to think in the context of their God-belief. We must help them process the information they already have, both intellectually *and emotionally* (starting from their God-concept), and we must be intentional and creative about it.

For instance, by the time a child reaches junior high school, he is well-acquainted with the question, "How does that make you feel?" We should ask the same question so that we can quickly follow up with an additional one: "How do you think that makes God feel?" We should intentionally, blatantly, and repeatedly link the two questions until our children can no longer hear the first question without thinking of the second. It should become an automatic internal response so that no matter where they are, the first question will always trigger the second question in their minds, bringing the focus back to God, not self. That is powerful linkage. In effect, the culture will help us do our job every time they ask the initial question, because we will have already preprogrammed our children how to respond to that question.

But we must also be creative in other ways. During our years at the University of Washington, my wife and I invited students to watch secular movies in our home on Friday nights.[52] We showed the whole spectrum of movies, from *Ground Hog Day* starring Bill Murray, to *Rope* by Alfred Hitchcock. Following the movie, we would ask questions to help students think through their own view of God and life and how it compared with the views portrayed in the movie.

We used a borrowed video projector so the picture covered the whole wall like in a theater, and we ran the sound through the stereo system. We served lots of pizza, popcorn, and soda, and made sure that we "entertained" the students. As a result, we packed the place out each week. Most importantly, we intellectually and emotionally inoculated and re-educated students who probably would have never come to a Christian Worldview class. We helped the students think through their belief system and the belief systems around them in a practical, fun, engaging, non-threatening *relational* way. Teaching about God using secular films is a bit unorthodox, but it was highly effective. We gave the students what they wanted: relationships, food, fun, and entertainment. In the process we also taught them what they needed: practical theology about the God of the Bible within their cultural context.

If we can *together*—teachers, musicians, business people, politicians, "soccer moms," and all other Christians with their respective platforms—link people's everyday beliefs to their God-belief, then we will be in a position to ultimately change both levels of belief by addressing the latter. The goal is to get the culture (both inside and outside the church) to debate "God" *in the context of everyday belief*, because that perceptually makes "God" more pertinent to their intellectual *and* emotional lives. We must help them rediscover God.

Building the Dike

Two things are absolutely necessary. First, leaders must surface across the nation who are willing to put everything on the line in order to accomplish the task—just as our Founding Fathers did. They must drive the process. Every national cause requires a leader. This is obvious in even a cursory reading of history.

William Wilberforce and the Clapham Sect in England are a good example of leaders with various gifts and resources banding together in pursuit of a God-given cause.

We need leaders in every community who will step forward and together lead the charge to make God the issue—first in their community, then in their state, and ultimately in the nation. If those individuals to whom God has given the platform, abilities, and resources to lead fail to do so, then who is going to lead?

Leaders should do three things: First, they must seek to reach their peers with the message of Jesus Christ. This creates a larger group of leaders who can move forward together. Second, they should use their platforms to reach everyone else in their spheres of influence, such as subordinates or other groups and audiences to whom they have access. Third, they should think creatively about how they may use their pooled influence to reach the culture around them. They can utilize television ads, newspaper ads, billboards, and campaigns springboarding off of various issues. They can go discretely as a group to the owner of a television or radio station in town asking for offensive material to be removed and replaced with more God-oriented programming (of course, incremental steps are acceptable).

> *If those individuals to whom God has given the platform, abilities, and resources to lead fail to do so, then who is going to lead?*

Leaders can recruit key state politicians to throw sand in the works of the budgets of targeted state universities and hold embarrassing public hearings (outwardly unrelated) for university officials and professors antagonistic toward God, in order to encourage a less hostile campus environment for those who wish to make God the issue. In most cases, the real agenda can be moved forward entirely below the radar of the media. Of course, with their alma maters, they can become heavily involved in leading, advising, and shaping the alumni associations. They can go to Christian groups on campus to help them figure out how to make God the issue in that university. In such a situation they can bring finances, top marketing people, and strategic planners to the table—as well as added accountability and encouragement. They can as a group strategically give (or withhold) money to influential local charities in order to encourage a more God-centric agenda. They can recruit and fund individuals to run for office who will seek to make God the issue by reshaping much of the cultural rhetoric and issues.

The possibilities are endless, but it must be done with the leverage of a group. Ten to twenty core group members who are individuals of influence in their communities are all that is really needed. Who will lead the effort to reestablish God's presence in the public square of America?

The second necessity is moving *together*. In politics. In business. In media. In entertainment. In education. If we are isolated we cannot stand for long, but together we can succeed. Solomon, the wisest man who ever lived, once said, "Though one may be overpowered, two can defend themselves. A cord of three strands is not quickly broken" (Ecclesiastes 4:12). Even Jesus, the God of the universe, always sent His disciples out in pairs, never alone. However, simply *working* together is not enough. Merely creating alliances of fellow travelers is insufficient. We must be of one mind and heart. In a cord of "three strands," the strings are intertwined, not merely parallel. They give each other strength. We must be of one heart and mind, *together* steeled for the battle. If we are not of one heart, we will not speak with one voice. If we do not speak with one voice, we will not be heard. If we are not heard, we cannot control the rhetorical field of battle. And if we cannot control the rhetorical battlefield, we will never make God the issue in our society.

If we are not of one heart, we will not speak with one voice. If we do not speak with one voice, we will not be heard.

A few years ago I heard the story of a fraternity pledge class in San Diego. The fraternity members took all the pledges down to the beach and built a fire. Each pledge was given a cup of water to throw on the fire. One at a time each pledge emptied the contents of his cup onto the flames—with little effect. But then each pledge's cup was refilled. They were instructed to circle the bonfire, and when the word was given they were all to simultaneously empty their cups of water on the fire. This time the fire was snuffed out. Acting alone is almost always shortsighted. Acting together is critical to success. Jesus sent His disciples out in pairs to teach us the folly of going it alone and the inherent strength that comes from moving ahead together.

Benjamin Franklin succinctly summed it up at the signing of the Declaration of Independence: "We must all hang together, or assuredly we shall all hang separately." If we wish to succeed, we must never act alone!

The only remaining issue is whether we will show up for the battle. Will we lead? Will we wholeheartedly commit or will we shrink back in the face of adversity? Will we rise above our own busyness or will distractions sideline us? Will we succumb to complacency or will we stand with those who were willing to die to get the message of the gospel through to us? It is a deliberate choice.

A number of years ago, Billy Graham shared a letter that an American college student had written to his fiancée, explaining why he was breaking off their engagement. Following is an excerpt of that letter:

> We communists have a high casualty rate. We live in virtual poverty, and turn back every penny we make to the Party above what is absolutely necessary to keep us alive. We communists don't have the time or the money for movies, concerts, or T-bone steaks or decent homes or new cars. I am in dead earnest. Communism is my life, my business, my religion, my sweetheart, my wife, my mistress, my bread and meat. I work at it in the daytime and dream about it at night. Its hold on me grows, not lessens, as time goes by. Therefore, I

cannot carry on a friendship, a love affair, or even a conversation without relating to this force which both drives and guides my life. I've already been in jail because of my ideas and if necessary I am ready to go before a firing squad.[53]

In 1951, an ambitious young California businessman wrote out a contract with God, agreeing to go anywhere and do anything God asked. And he meant it. He left himself no escape clauses—no wiggle room. And then he proceeded to live out his agreement. He started going to the local university campus to speak to students about Jesus. He recruited others to go with him. Five years later he sold his businesses to devote all of his time to evangelism and discipleship.

For over fifty years he never looked back. He never wavered. What he left in his wake was a movement of like-minded individuals who have touched over six billion people in virtually every corner of the world. Today, over 25,000 full-time and approximately 500,000 trained volunteer staff seek to tell everyone who will listen about the Good News of Jesus Christ in just about every country on the face of the earth. The name of the movement is Campus Crusade for Christ, and the name of the man was Bill Bright. God can do great things through anyone who will wholeheartedly commit to Him without reservation.

As I write this, the United States is waging war against Saddam Hussein in Iraq. I believe that the most significant story of this war is one that will probably never make the front page of the newspapers, but may well have a greater effect on Iraq in the next couple of decades than anything the United States does following this war. The Christian churches in Baghdad agreed that when the war came to their city, they would not flee along with their countrymen. They would not take their families to safety. Rather, they would stay in order to care for the wounded. They are deliberately putting their own lives and the lives of their children in harm's way in order to lift up the name of Jesus before the citizens of Baghdad. That is a symptom of wholehearted commitment to Jesus Christ.

When I was ten years old, a long-distance runner from Kenya by the name of Kipchoge "Kip" Keino astounded the world. I remember watching the Olympics that year with intense fascination as this relatively unknown, barefooted Kenyan went head-to-head with the world's best.

What I saw him do was incredible! He won the silver medal in the 5,000 meters, despite problems during the race, then won the gold in the 1,500 meters. But it was not until recently as I read a book by Pat Williams (of the Orlando Magic) that I learned the rest of the story. Following is Pat's narrative of Kip Keino:

> Kip Keino's first event was the five-thousand-meter race. Though he suffered from a gall-bladder infection and had trouble adjusting to the altitude in Mexico City, Keino ran courageously. Midway through the race, he faltered and collapsed with cramps. Though his

coach urged him to quit, Keino got up, shook off the cramps and finished the race—as a silver medallist.

After the race, Keino suffered from a great deal of pain, and his coach advised him to sit out the fifteen-hundred-meter event a few days later. The favored runner in the fifteen-hundred-meter race was Jim Ryun, of the United States, who was one of the best milers in the history of track and field events. Keino was told that he didn't stand a chance against Ryun. Nothing, though, could keep him from that track.

The day of the race, Keino was on his way from the hotel to the track when his taxi got stuck in traffic. He jumped out of the car and jogged the rest of the way to the stadium. By the time he arrived, he was winded, having already run over a mile before his one-mile event. He took his place at the starting line. Ryun lined up a few yards away. The gun sounded, and Keino seemed to shed this pain and weariness. He ran like the wind that blows across the Kenyan plains, and he beat Jim Ryun and won the gold medal.

Kipchoge "Kip" Keino runs with endurance, but the race he's most involved in is not measured in meters but in lives. The race Kip Keino cares about most is the human race. After winning the gold in Mexico City, he returned to Kenya and his job as a police officer.

Once, while on patrol, Keino came across three orphans who were living on the street and hadn't eaten in days. He took those three children into his own home and adopted them. Sometime later, he came across some more orphans. He took them home, too. People heard about Kip Keino's growing family of adopted kids, and they brought more children to him. Before long, he had turned a farm into a Christian children's home that houses nearly a hundred orphans and abandoned children.

On the track and in his life, Kip Keino knows how to endure like Jesus. When he suffers pain and obstacles, he refuses to be stopped or turned aside from his goal. He pushes past the pain, he hurdles over the opposition and he keeps on going. He ignores the advice of those who say, "Just quit. You've done all you can do."[54]

Like Kip Keino, Bill Bright, and the Christians in Iraq, God has given each of us a platform, abilities, resources— and opportunities. He has also given each of us a choice. May we ponder these poignant words of the Rev. Martin Niemöller, a pastor in Nazi Germany:

First they came for the Jews. I was silent. I was not a Jew. Then they came for the Communists. I was silent. I was not a Communist. Then they came for the trade unionists. I was silent. I was not a trade unionist. Then they came for me. There was no one left to speak for me.[55]

The choice we face today may not have the same consequences for us as it did for Rev. Niemöller, but it could. We do not know. But the words of Tammy Bruce, a lesbian and author of *The Death of Right and Wrong*, should haunt our thoughts: "Welcome to a culture where right and wrong have taken such a beating they're no longer recognizable. If you think this debasement of our culture can never really affect you, think again. Today's moral relativism and selfish agendas are moving through the body of society like a cancer, putting all of us at risk."[56]

What we do know is that the choices we make today will have consequences—for better or for worse. And we know that our children and grandchildren will have to live with the results of our choices.

Will we rise to the challenge or will we bury our heads in the sands of indifference, prosperity, and busyness until it is too late? If we chose not to make God the issue now, our grandchildren may never even have the opportunity to do so.

God is the issue. God is the watershed. He is the only one who can push back the raging tide of moral relativism and secularism. *If we fail to make God the issue, we shall most certainly and inevitably fail at all other related tasks*. Time is not on our side. May God grant us wisdom, courage, and strength for the journey ahead. May He grant us the privilege to help our fellow Americans once again rediscover the God of the Bible.

Review Questions

1. Drawing on the examples of platforms in this chapter, what platform(s) has God given you in our culture? To what degree have you acknowledged where He has put you as evidenced by your engagement with the culture?

2. What three things could you do within the next six months to take advantage of your platform and make God the issue in your circle of influence?

3. How many other Christians are there who share the same, or a similar, platform with whom you could combine efforts? What could you do to encourage a co-laboring effort among yourselves?

4. How does discovering a God-given platform relate to the idea of stewardship—being responsible to use what God has entrusted to us?

5. If God were to evaluate your life today for your impact in making Jesus Christ the focal point of American culture, what kind of evaluation do you think you would receive?

End Notes

1. George Washington, from his Farewell Address, September 19, 1796. Quoted in James D. Richardson, *A Compilation of the Messages and Papers of the Presidents, 1789–1897* (Published by Authority of Congress, 1899), Vol. I, p. 220.

2. Quoted in *America's God and Country Encyclopedia of Quotations*, compiled by William J. Federer (St. Louis, MO: FAME Publishing, 1999), p. 660.

3. John Adams in his address to the military, October 11, 1798. Quoted in Charles Francis Adams, ed., *The Works of John Adams —Second President of the United States* (Boston: Little, Brown, & Co., 1854), Vol. IX, p. 229.

4. Jane Clayson interview with Anne Graham Lotz, "The Early Show," September 13, 2001 (www.cbsnews.com/earlyshow/ healthwatch/healthnews/20010913terror_spiritual.shtml).

5. Andrew Sullivan, "The Conservative Case for Gay Marriage," *Time* magazine, June 30, 2003, p. 76.

6. Margaret Sanger from her personal writings. Quoted in Bill Bright, *Red Sky in the Morning* (Orlando, FL: NewLife Publications, 1998), p. 94.

7. Aldous Huxley, *Ends and Means* (Harper & Brothers, 1927), p. 315. Quoted by Os Guinness in *Time for Truth* (Grand Rapids, MI: Baker Books, 2002), p. 113.

8. Aleksandr Solzhenitsyn, "Warning to the West," delivered over the BBC radio network, March 24, 1976.

9. The illustration of patching the walls of the house was from a talk by Rev. Tony Evans at Campus Crusade for Christ's 1992 U.S. Staff Training conference.

10. Lest my words be misconstrued, I am not espousing a theocracy in any way, shape, or form. "Christianity" imposed by fiat, rather than freely embraced, is not Christianity at all. It would in fact be no better than the militant Islamic theocracies that enforce and advance outward adherence to Islam by the ruthless wielding of the sword.

11. Using a process called "linkage" (which I discuss in Chapter 3), the press has effectively linked the concept of stem-cell research with the use of embryos to find cures for various diseases. In reality, no such cures have come from the use of embryonic stem cells; on the contrary, all successes to date have been through the use of stem cells from adults or other nondestructive sources.

12. Steven Butts, "Pornography: A Serious Cultural Disorder That is Accelerating," *Lancaster Sunday News*, March 9, 1997. Quoted by James Dobson in *Bringing Up Boys* (Wheaton, IL: Tyndale House Publishers, 2001), p. 210.

13. George Barna, "Americans Are Most Likely to Base Truth on Feelings," *Barna Update*, Feb. 12, 2002.

14. George Barna, *Real Teens* (Ventura, CA: Regal Books, 2001), p. 131.

15. Ibid., p. 124.

16. Ibid., p. 132.

17. "2002 Report Card: The Ethics of American Youth," Josephson Institute of Ethics, October 20–26, 2002.

18. Ibid.

19. Oswald Chambers, *My Utmost for His Highest* (Westwood, NJ: Barbour & Company, Inc., 1935), p. 96.

20. Denise Keirnan, "Christian group won't allow gay student to be leaders," *The Daily of the University of Washington*, October 13, 1994, p. 1.

21. Jim Brünner, "Why is CCC's discrimination condoned by UW?" *The Daily of the University of Washington*, October 14, 1994, p. 4.

22. Martin Luther King, Jr., *Strength to Love* (Fortress, NY: Fortress Press, 1963).

23. Joseph Lieberman, from his address at Notre Dame University, October 24, 2000. Aired on *The News Hour with Jim Lehrer* on PBS on October 26, 2000.

24. "American Faith is Diverse, As Shown Among Five Faith-Based Segments," *The Barna Report*, January 29, 2002 (www.barna. org).

25. Bill Bright and Ron Jenson, *Kingdoms at War* (San Bernardino, CA: Here's Life Publishers, 1986), pp. 28–29.

26. Technically, they are "Positive Law" jurists who by definition believe that law is based solely upon prior law (case law) rather than on right and wrong. Therefore, in order to change law all they need do is find an obscure law or court decision that can be interpreted to show precedent for their view. Right and wrong, and by implication justice, have nothing to do with it.

27. For more information, read *More Than a Carpenter* and *Beyond Belief to Convictions* by Josh McDowell.

28. Saul D. Alinsky, *Rules for Radicals: A Pragmatic Primer for Realistic Radicals* (Vintage Books, 1989), p.136.

29. Quoted in *America's God and Country Encyclopedia of Quotations*, compiled by William J. Federer (St. Louis, MO: FAME Publishing, 1996), p. 676.

30. BBC News, "Erfurt massacre planned for months," April 30, 2002.

31. BBC News, "History of School Shootings," April 26, 2002.

32. According to abcNEWS.com, September 25, 2001, Cassie Bernall's friend, Michelle Fox, said, "Cassie was in the library study-

ing the Bible, as she did every day at lunch, when the shooting began. She knelt and prayed, which angered one of the shooters. But she continued to pray, so he shot her. 'I know she died because of her faith in God.'"

33. Quoted in *America's God and Country Encyclopedia of Quotations*, p. 540.

34. Mr. Blair was finally forced to resign May 1, 2003, only after the evidence was becoming too public to suppress any longer.

35. This argument also applies directly to the euthanasia (death with dignity/mercy killing) debate.

36. In most cases I would recommend bringing in someone from the outside to debate, since this is not a subject that most high school students are well equipped to handle.

37. Thomas Jefferson, November 16, 1798, in the Kentucky Resolutions of 1798, Article III. Quoted in *America's God and Country Encyclopedia of Quotations*, p. 323.

38. For more quotes by Thomas Jefferson regarding Church and State issues, see *America's God and Country Encyclopedia of Quotations*.

39. Joseph Lieberman, address at Notre Dame University, October 24, 2000. Aired on "The News Hour with Jim Lehrer" on PBS on October 26, 2000.

40. Barry Asmus, *When Riding a Dead Horse, for Heaven's Sake... Dismount!* (Marietta, GA: Ameripress, 1995).

41. "Infidel" refers to any non-Muslim. It can also be translated as "pagan," "disbeliever," or "idolater."

42. "What the World Thinks in 2002," The Pew Research Center for the People and the Press, December 4, 2002, p. 5.

43. Ibid.

44. An excellent video, *Unlocking the Mystery of Life: The Scientific Case for Intelligent Design*, which was aired by PBS, is available from Campus Crusade at www.goccc.com or 800-352-8273. Following are a few books that are well regarded: *Darwin on Trial* and *Defeating Darwinism* by Phillip Johnson, *Darwin's Black Box* by Michael Behe, and *Evolution: A Theory in Crisis* by Michael Denton.

45. *Reminiscences of Levi Coffin* (Cincinnati: Western Tract Society, 1876), p. 108.

46. On March 24, 1976, Aleksandr Solzhenitsyn gave a speech over the BBC radio network in which he stated that socialism cost the Soviet Union 110 million lives from 1917 to 1959.

47. To order a copy, go to www.Jesusfilm.org then click on "Resources," or call 800-432-1997.

48. Barry Asmus, a phenomenal communicator and one of the country's top economists, would be an excellent choice; he will gladly incorporate the spiritual dimension. Contact him at www.barryasmus.com or 480-596-3442. There are many other suitable speakers as well.

49. Bill Bright's book *GOD: Discover His Character* speaks directly to this issue. It has an accompanying workbook and training videos for group settings. To order, go to www.nlpdirect.com or call 800-235-7255.

50. George Barna, *Third Millennium Teens* (Ventura, CA: Barna Research Group, 1999), p. 39.

51. According to "Americans Are Most Likely to Base Truth on Feelings," *Barna Update* (Feb. 12, 2002), "Only 9% of born-again teens believe in moral absolutes." This would seem to clearly imply that the remaining 91% of born-again teens have an inaccurate view of God.

52. Note that in some cases a movie may need to be edited ahead of time. In such cases, tell students that it is edited so they do not innocently rent it thinking the movie is okay in its original form. You can do rough edits at home if you connect two VCRs; otherwise, you may need to find a technically inclined person who can help (possibly through your church).

53. Billy Graham, speech at Urbana 1957, InterVarsity Christian Fellowship / USA.

54. Pat Williams, *How to Be Like Jesus* (Deerfield Beach, FL: Health Communications, 2003), p. 252.

55. *Encyclopedia of the Holocaust* (New York: Macmillan Publishing Company, 1990).

56. Tammy Bruce, *The Death of Right and Wrong* (Roseville, CA: Prima Publishing, 2003), p.11.

About the Author

 BRAD BRIGHT is the youngest son of Bill and Vonette Bright, founders of Campus Crusade for Christ. Shortly after graduating from Wheaton College, Brad entered national politics as a result of both Watergate and studying the life of William Wilberforce. He worked as an aide to U.S. Senator William Armstrong of Colorado, as a deputy director of the National Republican Congressional Committee, and as director of a foundation to promote volunteerism as an alternative to federal government programs. In 1989 he joined the staff of Campus Crusade for Christ, where he has worked with both college students and national leaders. He is on the board of the Bill Bright Leadership Center and the Bright Media Foundation, and serves as the director of a new strategy called the "Discover God" movement, which seeks to reframe the God-concept of both Christians and non-Christians in America today. He resides in Orlando, Florida, with his wife, Kathy, and their two children.